For Parrish and Miranda

HEROIC WOMEN
OF THE ART WORLD
RISKING IT ALL FOR ART

Eugene H. Pool

For further information, contact:

Tumblehome, Inc. / 201 Newbury St, Suite 201 / Boston, MA 02116 / https://tumblehomebooks.org

Library of Congress Control Number 2019940376 / ISBN-13 978-1-943431-53-3 / ISBN-10 1-943431-53-1

Pool, Eugene, Heroic Women of the Art World / Eugene Pool - 1st ed

Book design by Yu-Yi Ling

Printed in Taiwan

10 9 8 7 6 5 4 3 2 1

CONTENTS

INTRODUCTION

"We have the responsibility as writers and artists to imagine the lives of others as a way to stand with them."— *Teju Cole*

During the Nazi occupation of Paris in World War II, museum curator Rose Valland risked her life daily to save thousands of art works stolen from Jewish families and French museums for Hitler's private collection. Across the Atlantic, Harlem sculptor Augusta Savage defied parental abuse, the death of two husbands, racism, and poverty, to produce a monumental sculpture that dominated the 1939 World's Fair in New York. Today, photographer Annie Leibovitz mixes courage and creativity covering foreign wars and genocide as well as celebrities like Channing Tatum and Lupita Nyong'o.

I call this book *"Heroic Women of the Art World"* for good reason. In a variety of art roles, the women in this book courageously risked everything, including their lives, for art. This remarkable bravery prompted me to gather their stories. They deserve to be widely known. Many of their stories have not been fully told, as they are here, and many of the illustrations of their art have never been seen in a book.

These women represent a diversity of cultures, races, ethnicities, countries of origin, sexual orientations, and historical periods. They also showcase the astonishing range of roles available to women in the art world. You can be a painter, sculptor, or architect—or even a video artist—but there are other paths, too. You can be a curator caring for art works in a museum. You can be a conservator, bringing damaged paintings back to life. You can be an activist like the masked Guerrilla Girls, demonstrating for women's rights. You can even be an art detective.

I'm sure you've heard of Rembrandt and Picasso. The first was an Old Master. The other was a 20th century genius. But both were men. The world of art has not, until recently, been very accepting to women. Now it's time to read about Maya Lin, Rosa Bonheur, Augusta Savage, Zaha Hadid, and the others. They come from many different places—Harlem, Iraq, Mexico, France, Italy, Great Britain, China, and of course the United States. But they share conviction, talent, and passion.

Maya Lin designed the Vietnam Veterans Memorial in Washington when she was just a college student. Pan Yuliang overcame poverty and racism to become an internationally recognized painter. French art cop Mireille Ballestrazzi, later head of INTERPOL (our global police organization), hunted down forgers, smugglers, and art thieves around the globe.

The personal lives of these women are varied. They were poor and rich, persecuted and privileged, famous one moment and forgotten the next, gay, bi, and straight, but always, always powerful arts women.

An art historian and author, I've been involved with great art all my life, growing up in a house with original works by Mary Cassatt, Vieira da Silva, Lee Krasner, Picasso, Modigliani, and others. After studying fine arts at Harvard, I taught art history classes at one of the nation's top private schools in Cambridge, Massachusetts and helped develop an innovative educational plan for youth at the Museum of Fine Arts, Boston. I studied design at the Boston Architectural College and painting under muralist Josh Winer. I loved working with students because they were so creative and optimistic.

I hope you'll be excited by the stories of the women in this book. May they remind you of the importance of art, expose you to the variety of careers available, introduce to you a wealth of role models, and encourage you to follow in their footsteps.

— April, 2019, Boston, Massachusetts

1. AN UNEXPECTED LIFE

Sofonisba Anguissola, Painter, Italy (1532-1625)

Twenty-something Sofonisba Anguissola stood quietly, hands folded, in the great room of the Mendoza family palace in Guadalajara, Spain. It was early February, 1560. Outside, the winter wind howled against the massive stone building. Shivering beneath the ornate gown she wore for the occasion, Anguissola missed the warmth and familiarity of her home with her parents and five sisters. Seven hundred miles from Cremona, Italy, she waited to meet the woman she been summoned to serve, the fiancée of the King of Spain.

Anguissola's father, Amilcare, had overturned her life by ordering her to the Spanish court. He said it was an opportunity for her painting to be noticed at the highest level. But Anguissola felt so alone. Did she have the strength to do this? Would she be able to stick it out in this strange place with these Spanish courtiers she did not know and whose language she did not understand? Could she make her father proud? Or would she have to go home, disappointing him?

Standing in small groups, the men and women suddenly hushed their whispers. All eyes turned to the far end of the room as Elisabeth de Valois entered. She was just fourteen. The French girl had come to marry thirty-two-year-old King Philip II of Spain, who had lost two wives already. As courtiers guided her across the room, gentlemen and ladies bowed and curtsied, their silks rustling in the echoing room.

Isabel, as she was called in Spain, wore a black velvet gown embroidered with flowers and a white linen ruff that rose as high as her ears. The dress was much fancier than the drab wear of the Spanish ladies. She stopped before Anguissola, and the painter curtsied.

Self-Portrait at the Easel, (detail).

Then, rising, Anguissola lifted her eyes to the queen's face. Their gazes met. Sofonisba saw before her a slight girl, with dark eyebrows and hair in tight curls that, against her pale skin, gave her a striking but fragile look.

For her part, Isabel saw a petite woman with fine auburn hair in a French braid, a round face, pink cheeks, and pale green eyes. The painter's peaceful expression immediately made the child queen feel comfortable. Like the painter, Isabel, too, was far from home, which was six hundred miles away in Blois. She, too, had left behind the warmth of family, her mother Catherine de Medici and her best friend Mary Stuart, the teenaged Queen of Scots. Isabel and her mother had both dissolved in tears at the Spanish border, where Catherine halted to let her daughter go on alone to her new husband and country. A worse separation followed. Isabel's father held a joust celebrating his daughter's wedding, but an opponent's splintered lance pierced his left eye and entered his brain, killing him instantly.

In the great, cold room Anguissola and Isabel trembled alike with anxiety, anticipation, and hope. Surrounded by older men and women they did not know, hearing the different language of a new land, the two young women embarked on a phase of life that would lead to an unanticipated but deep friendship. For Anguissola, this unlikely relationship was just the first of several surprising developments in what turned out to be a thoroughly unexpected life.

* * *

Sofonisba Anguissola was born in Cremona, Italy, probably in 1532. The Anguissolas lived in a small stone *palazzo* with an interior courtyard. It was a lively, busy household. Amilcare, a nobleman and widower with a son as well as the six girls, made sure their days were filled. For the girls there was not only chess to play, but also drawing, painting, and embroidery to learn, and music, Latin, and literature, from tutors who came on a tight schedule. By the time she was a teen Anguissola was accomplished at all these subjects, but particularly at the easel. As a painter, she already stood apart.

In Anguissola's day, there were no art schools. Aspiring artists apprenticed to masters when they were young, sometimes only seven or eight years old. But apprentices were all male. As a female, Anguissola couldn't follow this path. It was considered inappropriate for a girl to be exposed to the sometimes-nude models that artists painted. Furthermore, it was said the work was too hard. Finally, Anguissola was nobility; aristocrats simply didn't work. Still, her father knew Sofonisba and her sisters were talented, so he found them their own personal art teacher. When Sofonisba was just twelve, he sent her and her sister Elena to live and study with the artist Bernardino Campi. They stayed for three years.

As an artist, Anguissola was extraordinarily gifted. While five of the six Anguissola girls—Lucia, Anna Maria, Elena, Europa, and Sofonisba herself—became professional painters, Sofonisba was so much better that in 1554, when

Anguissola Family Portrait, showing Asdrubale and Minerva with their father Amilcare.

she was just twenty-two, she was trading drawings with the greatest artist in the world, Michelangelo. The man who painted the Sistine Chapel in Rome and sculpted the muscular *David* in Florence sent her sketches to copy and color for practice. Sofonisba sent him drawings to show how she was progressing. One of the funniest and most famous shows her baby brother. A crayfish the size of a small lobster has just nipped his finger, and Asdrubale is crying his head off. A little girl in the picture—probably their sister Minerva—wraps a comforting arm about him, but she also can't help laughing. It's the kind of real-life family scene that Anguissola was particularly good at.

So was the lively *The Chess Game*, understandably Sofonisba's most popular painting. Three of her five sisters and their governess gather around a chess-board. Lucia, Europa, and Minerva laugh as they play together. What fun they're having! As Lucia puts her hand on a piece, she looks out at us as if to say, "Watch this move!" It must have been a good one because Minerva, her opponent, lifts a hand in shock. Little Europa at the back giggles at Minerva's dis-comfort.

The painting truly shows off the sisters and the kind of people they were. Three smart girls wearing beautiful velvet dresses thinking hard,

The Chess Game.

playing well, and having fun. And the girls look realistic and full of personal-ity. As the famous art biographer Giorgio Vasari said, Anguissola's figures here were "all done with such care and such spirit, that they have all the appearance of life, and are wanting in nothing save speech."

But now Anguissola had traded her family for a royal court and a woman she knew little about. Anguissola spoke a little French, Isabel a little Italian. When they first met, on that bitter February morning, they exchanged a few words. Then smiles appeared on both sides. They felt an instant bond. *You're an artist*, Isabel might have thought. *I'm an artist, too.* She sketched with chalk pencils and painted, although she was just a beginner. Anguissola was, of course, a successful professional, having executed portraits for many people in Italy. *You're a young woman far from home, missing your family*, Anguissola might have thought. *So am I.* For Anguissola, Isabel was another sister to replace the four younger sisters she had left behind. For Isabel, Anguissola was an older sister like Mary, and a friend with whom she shared a common interest. And each knew the other played the clavichord.

Soon they were spending long, happy hours together as art teacher and pupil. One courtier wrote of them, "The queen, who shows much ingenuity, has begun to paint, and Anguissola, who is a great favorite of hers, says that she draws in a naturalistic way in a fashion in which it appears that she knows well the person whom she is painting." Slowly Anguissola and Isabel became, amid the austere, somber court of Spain, each other's companions in art, music, and life—best friends.

For Anguissola, no role could have suited her better. She didn't want to just marry, because if she did, her attention would go to her husband, not her art. She couldn't be a nun, because she wouldn't be allowed to paint. And as a nobleman's daughter, she wasn't permitted to hold an actual job. But at the Spanish court, appointed court painter as well as Isabel's lady in waiting, she could continue to use her artistic talent while enjoying the companionship of a good friend.

Anguissola was, in fact, the only woman in European history to enjoy such a position. Over the years she produced numerous individual and group portraits of the Spanish royal family, though always in more formal dress and poses than she used in her earlier Italian pictures. Her portrait of Don Carlos, Philip's son by an early marriage, was so popular thirteen copies were made for various family members. King Philip clearly appreciated her ability. He took very good care of her, treating her well and making sure that the court, lords and ladies both, honored her. He made sure that she was given jewelry, money, and fine clothes. He promised her a substantial dowry and, whenever she was ready, an arranged marriage to a suitable nobleman. As biographer Vasari put it, "He keeps her with a rich allowance about the person of the Queen, to the admiration of all that Court, which reveres the excellence of Anguissola as a miracle...." Anguissola was that unusual woman of her time who supported herself entirely on her own.

Anguissola painted Queen Isabel's portrait several times. She painted the most prominent version, now in the Prado Museum in Madrid, in 1563 when she was thirty-one and the queen just seventeen. It shows Isabel in a long, black, velvet dress decorated with rubies and pearls. White silk undersleeves are decorated with gold. Isabel wears a jeweled collar called a *carcanet* below a crisp ruff, and a tiara of more rubies and pearls. Her luminous skin shows off her dark hair and eyes. It's a formal court portrait, unlike those of Anguissola's sisters, so Isabel stands straight and still. In her right hand she shows a tiny locket portrait of Philip. But likely because she and Anguissola were so close, a hint of a smile plays on her lips.

Anguissola sent a different portrait of Isabel to Pope Pius IV in Rome, who had heard of the artist's work and requested a picture. In Anguissola's modest note she wrote: "From the very reverend Nuncio of your Holiness I understood that you desired to have a portrait by my hand of her Majesty the Queen, my Liege-lady. I send it to you, and, if I shall have satisfied therein the desire of your Holiness, I shall receive infinite compensation; but I must not omit to tell you that if it were possible in the same way to present with the brush to the eyes of your Holiness the beauties of the mind of this most gracious Queen, you would see the most marvelous thing in all the world...."

Although Isabel's and Philip's marriage was arranged for political reasons, and Isabel was younger than the king by eighteen years, the two grew fond of

Isabel de Valois.

each other. Sadly, Isabel suffered a miscarriage of twin girls in 1564. However, on August 12, 1566 she gave birth to a healthy girl, Isabella Clara Eugenia, and on October 10, 1567, to Isabella's sister, Catarina Michaela. But on October 3, 1568 a second miscarriage resulted in Isabel's death. Philip was devastated. Anguissola, too, was heartbroken. Now thirty-six, she stayed on at the court, committed to Isabel's two girls, honoring the memory of her close friend.

Two years later Philip kept his promise to Anguissola, producing a dowry of 3,000 *ducados* and a nobleman for a husband, Don Fabrizio de Moncada, Viceroy of Sicily, whom Anguissola married, in either 1570 or 1571. By this time

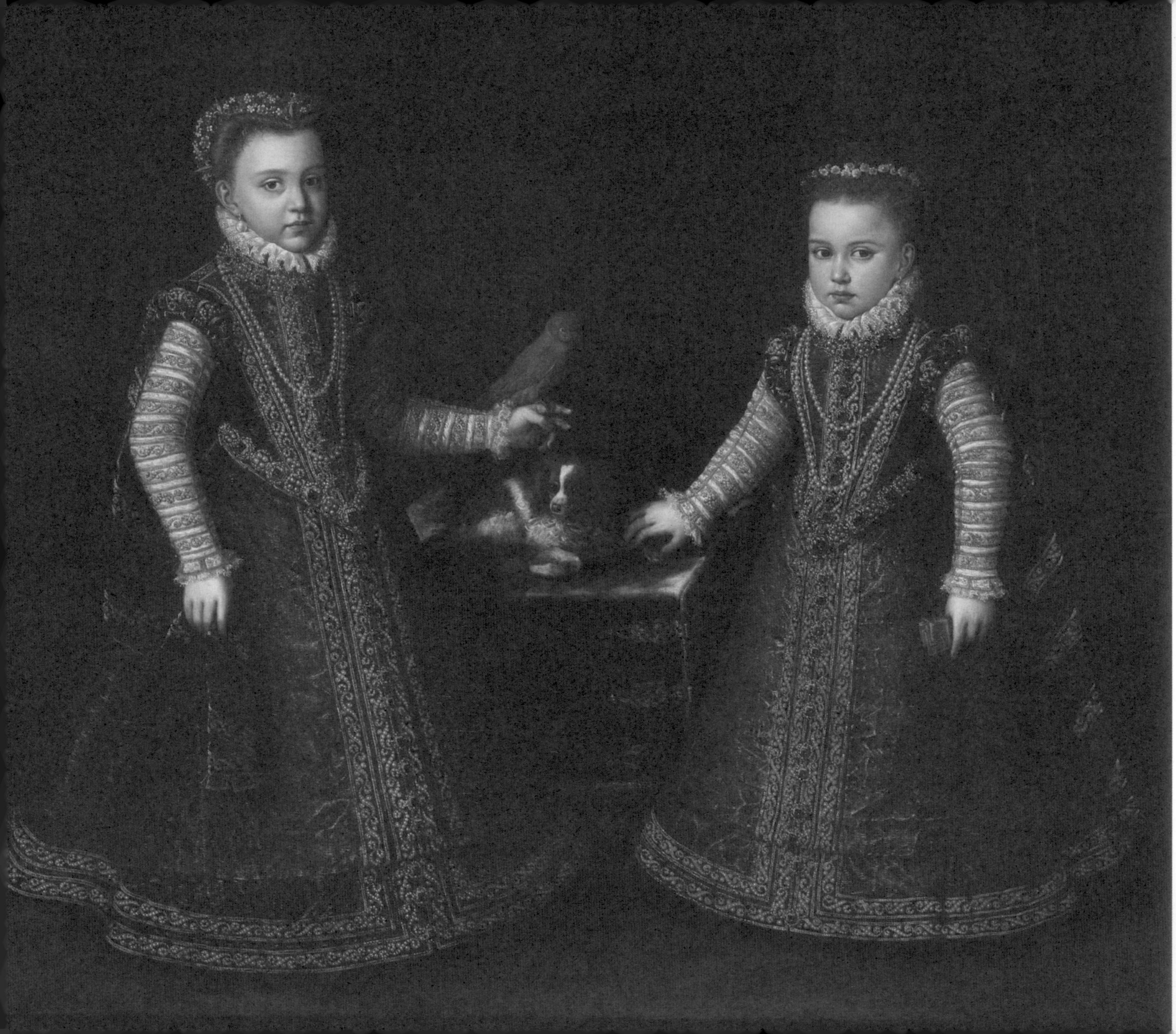

Isabel's Daughters.

she was independently quite wealthy from what she had earned, saved, and received as gifts.

The couple remained at the court for several years, departing in 1578, when Anguissola was forty-six, after she had spent some twenty years in Spain. By now Isabella and Catarina were young women. Anguissola settled with Fabrizio in Palermo, Sicily, where he had a *palazzo*. Unfortunately, Fabrizio died only a year later, perhaps in a shipwreck but more likely from the plague that periodically visited Sicily.

One cold January morning in 1580, Anguissola set sail from Palermo for Naples, the first leg of a long journey to Cremona, to return to her family's home. The captain of the ship was Orazio Lomellino, a nobleman and merchant from the coastal city of Genoa. During the sea passage, as one biographer described it, "love blossomed, their personalities pleased each other, the occasion was right, and she agreed to a second marriage." It was all very spontaneous. And Anguissola proposed to Orazio. This was absolutely unheard of, but the noble captain cheerfully accepted.

Since Anguissola's father Amilcare had died, her brother Asdrubale was now head of the Cremona household. Believing his sister was acting hastily, Asdrubale forbade her to marry Orazio. But Anguissola was used to being independent. She simply ignored Asdrubale, wedding Orazio a few weeks later at the age of forty-eight.

The couple took up residence in Genoa, where Anguissola continued to paint portraits, also trying her hand at Biblical scenes.

Her reputation was now international, and her home became a gathering place for artists and a must visit for the famous. It's likely that the great Flemish painter Peter Paul Rubens stopped by when he was traveling in the region. In 1599 the princess Isabella, her old friend Isabel's daughter, made a special detour to Genoa on her way from Spain to the Netherlands, where she had become the new queen, just to see Anguissola and have her portrait painted.

Eventually Orazio gave up his sea travels, and the artist and her husband retired to Palermo. Here another famous Flemish visitor was the artist Anthony van Dyck, who sketched Anguissola and painted two portraits. By then she was ninety-two and losing her sight. She had to hold pictures right up to her face to make them out.

Sofonisba Anguissola died a year after those final portraits, on November 16, 1625.

Unexpectedly, the little girl from the small town who couldn't go to art school shone in a foreign court far from home. In fact, Anguissola became an international art celebrity. Nearly four hundred years later, her work hangs in some of the most famous art museums in the world, including the Gardner in Boston, Prado in Madrid, and Uffizi in Florence.

Fame, friendship, wealth, love—Anguissola earned them all. Which would she have valued most? We can't know for sure, but we do know how strongly Orazio felt about her. On Anguissola's one hundredth birthday, he had an inscription incised on her tomb in the little stone church of San Giorgio dei Genovesi in Palermo: "To Anguissola, my wife, whose parents are the noble Anguissola, for beauty and extraordinary gifts of nature, who is recorded among the illustrious women of the world, outstanding in portraying the images of man, so excellent that there was no equal in her age. Orazio Lomellino, in sorrow for the loss of his great love, in 1632, dedicates this little tribute to such a great woman."

Self-Portrait at the Easel, Painting.

2. ARTEMISIA'S REVENGE

Artemisia Gentileschi, Painter, Italy (1593-1653)

Rome, 1612: Artist Agostino Tassi didn't really expect his nineteen-year-old student Artemisia Gentileschi to resist when he tried to rape her in her bedroom in her father Orazio's house, where he was supposed to be teaching her about linear perspective. After all, he was a good friend of Orazio. But Artemisia did fight back with her fists and a knife.

And police officials didn't really expect the young woman to stick to her story when they interrogated and tortured her, as they did every witness they doubted, after her father brought charges against Tassi. But Artemisia did.

As she described the assault to the judge at Tassi's trial, "He grabbed me by the waist, threw me on the bed, closed the door of the room and embraced me to rape me and take away my virginity. Even though I struggled for a while, the struggling went on until eleven o'clock, since he had come after dinner as

I said in my other testimony, to which I refer. And the bed post was what protected me until that hour, since I was holding tight and turned towards it."

Eventually Tassi overpowered her. Nonetheless, she testified, immediately after, "when I saw myself free, I went to the table drawer and took a knife and moved towards Agostino saying, 'I'd like to kill you with this knife because you have dishonored me.' He opened his coat and said: 'Here I am,' and I threw the knife at him and he shielded himself; otherwise, I would have hurt him and might easily have killed him."

Self-Portrait as the Allegory of Painting.

* * *

Born July 8, 1593, Artemisia at nineteen was a broad-shouldered young woman with strong arms, abundant dark hair, and a direct, no-nonsense manner. She had large, brown, intelligent eyes. Because her mother, Prudentia Monotone, died when Artemisia was twelve, her father brought her up.

To the public, the seven-month rape trial was a riveting soap opera. For Artemisia, it was ongoing humiliation. The judge subjected her to a pelvic examination by two midwives, conducted while a notary observed. They affirmed she was not a virgin. Then officials tested the strength of her story. Interrogating witnesses, with the *sibille*, involved weaving a cord through metal bands around the base of the fingers, then slowly tightening the rope. The process could of course damage tendons or break bones. In Artemisia's case, it might have permanently crippled her hands so she could no longer hold a brush. As part of the interrogation, and as they were applying the *sibille*, the officials brought in Tassi. Under intense pressure from Orazio, Tassi promised to marry her to salvage her honor. But he never meant to do so. As he came before her, and officials painfully tightened the cords on her fingers, Artemisia famously spat at him, "So, *this* is the ring you give me?"

Where did Gentileschi find the courage to insist on justice in her case? She was already an accomplished painter who knew her own worth. In fact, at age seventeen, she had completed a painting of the Old Testament story of Susanna and the Elders that was a mature work by any standard. Two old men spy on Susanna, a married woman bathing in her garden. Gentileschi's painting shows the voyeurs leaning over a stone bench where a naked Susanna is trying to cover herself from their gaze. In the Biblical story the men demand that she have sex with them. If she won't, they say, they'll tell everyone they saw her with another man. Susanna refuses them, and the men carry out their threat. However, the young prophet Daniel interrupts her trial for adultery to insist that the two elders be questioned separately. Inconsistencies in their stories reveal they are lying. They, not Susanna, are punished. The woman in the story triumphs. Perhaps Susanna's story gave Gentileschi the courage to demand justice in her own case.

Tassi was a brutal man. He had raped his own sister-in-law (for which he was briefly jailed). When his wife left him, he put out a contract on her. In his defense during the rape trial, he produced six witnesses whose common theme was that Artemisia was a "whore" who had sex with everybody. Artemisia herself had just one defender, Giovanni Battista Stiattesi, a former friend of Tassi's. According to historian Elizabeth S. Cohen, he "reports Tassi's scheming and womanizing and alleges his hiring assassins to rid himself of his unfaithful wife. Further, sharing a bed with the witness one night, the painter had confessed to deflowering Artemisia and to promising marriage. Obligations, however, prevented Agostino [Tassi] from following through. His wife, who had run off with another man, was perhaps still alive."

The judge apparently didn't believe the testimony of either Tassi or his confederates. However, his resolution was to offer the artist an easy choice: five years' hard labor or exile from Rome. Of course Tassi chose the second option. Even so, he managed to get himself back to Rome, no problem, four months later.

But as for Artemisia, what was she to do? After the assault on her body, the public name-calling, the injustice of the outcome? How could she continue as a person and an artist in Rome? The answer lay in her amazing inner drive. Artemisia would not be defeated.

Susanna and the Elders.

Orazio quickly arranged a marriage, to save Artemisia's social reputation. Pietro Antonio di Vicenzo Stiattesi was also a painter and perhaps a relative of the Stiattesi who had supported Artemisia during the trial. And as soon as the couple could, in 1614, when Gentileschi was twenty-one, they moved to Florence. There, in Stiattesi's native city, Gentileschi hoped to make a new start.

Even before leaving for Florence, Gentileschi completed what many consider her signature painting, *Judith Beheading Holofernes*. Many artists had painted the scene, in which the Jewish heroine, to save her city from destruction by the Assyrian army, steals into the tent of its general Holofernes and decapitates him. However, no artist painted it with Artemisia's intensity.

The focus on the action is tight. The artist doesn't even show us the interior of the tent, just the bed on which Judith and her maidservant have pinned the general. Grabbing a fistful of his hair with one hand, with the other Judith saws at his neck with a sword. He fights for his life in vain. Blood splashes over the sheets. Judith leans back to avoid it. The bed, the violence, the struggle between man and woman—all these of course recall Gentileschi's rape. Only this time, the women have the power. No longer relying on men, they take justice, revenge, and their fates into their own hands.

One of two versions Gentileschi painted now hangs in the famous Uffizi Gallery in Florence. Hung in a darkened room, it still surprises tourists with its violence. They gasp out loud. The wall card doesn't mention the personal story

Judith Beheading Holofernes.

behind it, but the life-size figures are truly frightening.

Gentileschi's transition to Florence was remarkably smooth considering she was neither a native of the city nor a man. But she was a precocious talent, a far better painter than her own father. Not only extraordinarily talented, she was also a friend of Michelangelo Buonarroti the Younger, grandnephew of *the* Michelangelo. He, too, lived in Florence. Commissioning Gentileschi for a ceiling fresco at the Casa Buonarroti, where the master lived for a time, he paid her three times what he paid anyone else. He knew how good her work was. Even more remarkable, in an action indicative of the esteem in which she was held, the all-male Accademia dell' Arte del Designo (Academy of Art and Design) elected Gentileschi a member, the first woman ever to be so honored.

Cosimo II de Medici, Grand Duke of Tuscany, steered commissions her way. At his request, in fact, she painted the Uffizi version of the decapitation of Holofernes. Gentileschi established her reputation in the highest artistic and social circles. The great Galileo, who had come to Florence to escape the Inquisition, was among her friends. She continued to refine her style, employing more complex colors—such as purples and oranges—, subtler lighting, and more elegant clothes for her subjects. And Gentileschi continued to choose physically strong, commanding models for her women. *The Penitent Magdalene* and *Judith and Her Maidservant* are from this period. She also shed her husband, who had run up sizable gambling debts. Instead, she may have taken one Francesco Maringhi as a lover.

On August 2, 1617, when she was twenty-four, Gentileschi gave birth to a daughter, Prudentia (also known as Palmira). The girl went on to become a painter like her mother, although her works have been lost. Later Gentileschi may have had a second daughter, whose father may have been a priest. Accurate records from the period are rare. The names of the father and this child, likely born around 1625, are unknown. We know only that the artist married off two daughters with dowries, in 1636 and 1649.

In 1620 Gentileschi relocated to Genoa, invited by her father, who had commissions there. She not only assisted Orazio with paintings of Cleopatra and

Lucretia, but also met the Flemish artist Anthony van Dyck, who worked in the cool, crisp Northern manner Gentileschi began to admire.

A year later, now twenty-eight, she moved to Venice, then the next year, to Rome. Like any artist of the era, Gentileschi had to go wherever she could find commissions. In Rome the scholar and collector Cassiano dal Pozzo became her patron. For him she painted her famous *Self-Portrait as the Allegory of Painting*, now at England's Windsor Castle. It is one of the earliest images of a female artist actually at work. Gentileschi's powerful figure fills the frame, wearing a dress of green silk. A pendant on a gold chain is her only jewelry. Strands of dark hair spill down her forehead and cheek, giving the clear message that appearance is secondary to how she is going to place her next brushstroke. Light spills over her face and throat as, leaning forward, she lifts her brush, concentrating on a canvas that's just out of view. From the palette held low in her left hand, up through the arc of her poised body, to the powerful, bared right arm and raised hand grasping the brush between thumb and forefinger, the dynamic energy of her action is breathtaking.

Critic Whitney Chadwick explains that Gentileschi "has given herself the attributes of the female personification of Painting: the gold chain, the pendant mask standing for imitation, the unruly locks of hair that signify the divine frenzy of artistic creation, and the garments of changing colors which allude to the painter's skill."

A later *Mary Magdalene* from 1630.

By 1630 Gentileschi, now thirty-seven, was in Naples. She did not like the hot, noisy, crowded city, but as art historian Mary Garrard points out, "Like Rome in the early sixteenth century, or New York in the twentieth, Naples was the major art capital, a magnet for artists seeking opportunity and success." Not that Gentileschi really needed recognition by this time. A commemorative medal cast while she was still in Rome wraps her portrait with the words, "ARTEMISIA GENTILESCA PICTRIX CELEBRIS" (Artemisia Gentileschi, Celebrated Painter). But she was always willing to travel to get work.

This inclination took her to England in 1638. Now forty-five, she relocated once again to work with her father. Perhaps Gentileschi saw this as her last chance to paint with the seventy-five year old Orazio. And while she had executed commissions for the royal courts of both France and Spain, this opportunity

Corisca and the Satyr, c. 1635.

involved work on the Queen of England's very own residence in Greenwich: nine canvases for the ceiling of the great hall. The theme, "An Allegory of Peace and the Arts Under the English Crown," was to showcase the beneficent effects of the reign of Charles I and Henrietta Maria on their people. Three of the substantial-looking Muses—Clio, Terpsichore, and Polyhymnia—are almost certainly by Artemisia's hand alone.

After Orazio died on February 7, 1639, Gentileschi left England to return to Naples. Here the artist spent the rest of her life. Her patron was Don Antonio Ruffo of Messina, who also collected the artists Van Dyck, Poussin, and Rembrandt. Major works Gentileschi completed during this period include a *David and Bathsheba* and (if not by her, perhaps by one of her daughters) a *Lucretia*. A letter to Ruffo shows the toughness that enabled her to prevail over rape, a failed marriage, single motherhood, gender discrimination, and the challenges of self-employment. Requesting an advance of fifty ducats for two paintings, she was right up front about the issue: "These are paintings with nude figures requiring very expensive female models, which is a big headache for me. When I find good ones they fleece me, and at other times, one must suffer their trivialities with the patience of Job."

Artemisia Gentileschi died in Naples, probably in 1653 at age sixty, after a year of failing health. Or perhaps her death came later, in 1656, when a plague ravaged the city. She is believed to have been buried in the church of San Giovanni dei Fiorentini, destroyed when the neighborhood was "renewed" after World War II bombings. Her tombstone was reported by contemporary observers to have borne the simple legend "HIC ARTIMISIA" (Here is Artemisia).

A truly remarkable artist and strong character, with a style nearly as powerful and dark as the great Caravaggio himself, Gentileschi eclipsed the men who briefly loomed over her life. No one now remembers Antonio Tassi, who ended up a minor painter of frescoes for private palazzos. Only specialists know the work of Orazio.

By contrast, the paintings of Orazio's daughter hang in the famous Prado, Uffizi, Capodimonte, and Metropolitan museums, the Palazzo Pitti, and England's Royal Collection. In 1997 French film director Agnès Merlet made a feature film about her, called simply *Artemisia.* In 2002 Cathy Caplan wrote and directed a Manhattan play, "Lapis Blue Blood Red," based on Gentileschi's life. In 2011 the city of Milan honored her with a one-woman show at the Palazzo Reale. And in December, 2017, the Drouot auction house in Paris sold Gentileschi's *Self-Portrait as St. Catherine* for €2.3 million, more than five times its estimate.

Against so many odds, Artemisia Gentileschi prevailed.

3. PAINTER TO THE GUILLOTINED

Elisabeth Vigée Le Brun, Painter, France (1755-1842)

If she had waited any longer, agents of the Reign of Terror would have dragged thirty-four-year-old Elisabeth Vigée Le Brun and her nine-year-old daughter off to the guillotine and beheaded them. The date was October 5, 1789. The French Revolution was in full swing. A bloodthirsty mob had just hauled King Louis XVI and Marie Antoinette out of their palace at Versailles. As the queen's official portrait painter, Elisabeth Vigée Le Brun was a prime target for angry revolutionaries.

Vigée Le Brun hustled Julie out of their Paris home on Rue de Cléry into a midnight stagecoach. It clattered through the dark, cobblestone streets, headed out of the city. Disguised in servant's clothes, Vigée Le Brun hid her face behind a kerchief. In her autobiography, *Souvenirs*, she writes: "I had to leave several portraits unfinished, among others that of Mlle. Contat; I also refused to paint Mlle. de Laborde (now Duchesse de Noailles), who was brought to me by her

Self-Portrait in a Straw Hat.

father; she was scarcely sixteen and quite charming, but it was no longer a question of success or fortune, it was simply a matter of saving one's head."

Vigée Le Brun and her daughter had to get out of Paris without being noticed and captured. The artist was terrified a street mob would stop the coach and drag them onto the cobbles. As protection her husband Jean-Baptiste and her brother Robert rode with them. Luckily, as the coach crossed the city, the streets were empty and the neighborhoods quiet. Apparently, Elisabeth Vigée Le Brun concluded, "All the inhabitants, workers and the rest, had been to Versailles to fetch the Royal Family, and the fatigue following the journey kept them all safely asleep."

At the city limits Vigée Le Brun said a tearful farewell to her husband and brother. As she and Julie traveled on by themselves, Vigée Le Brun left behind husband, brother, house, career, and country. The ride was horrific. "Opposite me in the coach sat a very dirty man; he stank like the plague and told me quite simply that he had stolen some watches and other personal effects.... The thief was not content just to tell us about his noble deeds but spoke continually of stringing up this person and that person, naming a crowd of people I knew personally." Vigée Le Brun begged the man to stop.

"I cannot tell what I felt on crossing the Beauvoisin Bridge [into Sardinia, part of present-day Italy]. Only then did I start to breathe. I was out of France...."

Vigée Le Brun had with her just a few coins and her reputation as a portrait painter. She was a thirty-four-year-old woman, broke, on her own in a foreign country. As a single mother, wanted by powerful enemies, how was she to keep herself and her daughter alive?

Fortunately, Vigée Le Brun was a superb artist who loved to work. In *Souvenirs* she noted, "painting and living have always been one and the same thing for me." This passion for painting—and her talent—gave her a fighting chance in the years ahead.

* * *

Elisabeth Vigée Le Brun was born in 1755. Since women in Paris, where her family lived, were not admitted to art schools, she received her first training from her father. Louis Vigée was a successful painter to the upper class. He and Elisabeth were very close. Louis died suddenly in 1767 of an infection following surgery to remove a fish bone he'd swallowed. His death was a huge blow for his daughter, who was only twelve at the time. She and her father had shared

Vigée Le Brun and her daughter, Julie.

not only their skill in painting but also an ebullient temperament that allowed them to connect easily with people and win clients. Not until 1769, when Elisabeth was fourteen, did she receive formal art training. She studied with the history painter Gabriel Briard at his studio in the famous Louvre museum. Here she also made a fast friend, artist Rosalie Bocquet, who later lost her life to the guillotine.

By twenty-one the clearly talented Vigée Le Brun was already winning commissions for portraits. The painting of Marie Antoinette that she completed in 1783, when she was just twenty-eight, endeared her to the queen. Dressed in an elaborate gown, Marie Antoinette floats in folds of pale satin, as if on a cloud.

As an artist Vigée Le Brun came of age during the Rococo period of art, when lightness of touch, color, and subject matter were the style. Boucher and Fragonard were the popular painters. Artists no longer depicted historical events, classical gods or goddesses, or dramatic moments in nature, but

Queen Marie Antoinette of France.

instead rosy, mythical nymphs bathing in streams, aristocrats in fancy suits and dresses playing love games in gardens, and plump little *putti* infants romping with ribbons. Turquoise, saffron, and rose were the dominant colors. Vigée Le Brun's portrait of Marie Antoinette fit right in. And the artist had a sophisticated command of line, light, figure, facial expression, and color. Her smooth, accomplished portraits always made her subjects look their best.

Marie Antoinette thought so highly of the portrait she had two copies made, one for her brother Joseph II of Austria and the other for Catherine the Great of Russia, her brother's good friend. Vigée Le Brun went on to paint over twenty-five portraits of the queen, in both formal and informal dress. The painter genuinely liked the monarch, who encouraged the young artist, eventually appointing Vigée Le Brun as her official portraitist. In 1783 the queen even helped her get elected to the prestigious Académie Royale de Peinture et de Sculpture (Royal Academy of Painting and Sculpture) over the opposition of conservative male members.

However, when the stagecoach crossed the border, Vigée Le Brun reached the end of that chapter of her life. The imprisoned queen of France could no longer help her. She had to make up the rest of her story alone. The revolutionaries back in Paris assumed anyone leaving the country was an enemy, so they kept track of just who emigrated and why. To protect her own life and Julie's, Elisabeth needed to give the impression that she was simply on an art tour of the great museums of Europe, not trying to escape capture—and the guillotine. So she first headed for the city of Turin, which had a famous art museum.

The husband she left behind, Jean-Baptiste-Pierre Le Brun, was an art dealer and painter, though nowhere near as accomplished as his wife. He was an effective businessman but also a "spendthrift, womanizer, and inveterate gambler." Because Jean-Baptiste was a close friend of Jacques-Louis David, the painter in charge of the arts during the Revolution, he managed to remain in Paris during the Reign of Terror, retaining their home on Rue de Cléry.

After Turin, Vigée Le Brun traveled on to Parma, where Count Flavigny, a former minister of Louis XVI, welcomed her as his guest and ensured she was elected a member of its Academy. She continued on to Bologna and Florence, where she painted her most famous self-portrait, now in the Uffizi Gallery's restricted Vasari Corridor. The Grand Duke himself, another brother of Marie Antoinette, personally invited her to make this addition to the Gallery.

In the painting Vigée Le Brun shows herself at her easel, portraying Marie Antoinette. The artist wears a black dress, white ruff and cap, and red sash. Pausing in her work to look at us, Vigée Le Brun sits upright, brush in hand, a smile on her lips, clearly proud of herself as a professional hard at work.

December, 1789 found Vigée Le Brun in Rome, where she hoped not only to see great art works but also to find clients for portraits. She was not disappointed. Other French émigrés were living in the city. Her association with Marie Antoinette was a plus, not a minus. She loved visiting the Forum, the Capitoline Hill, and other sites of Roman history. Nonetheless Vigée Le Brun was homesick for France. Always. After all, it was her native country, where she had struggled to establish herself in a world dominated by men and succeeded.

Ever on the move, Vigée Le Brun arrived in Naples in the summer of 1790. She took a seaside villa at Chiaja, from which she had a view of the famously beautiful isle of Capri, and became friends with Queen Maria Carolina, Marie Antoinette's eldest sister. Once again Vigée Le Brun found many customers. She completed a lively portrait of a popular opera composer, Giovanni Paisiello.

By 1792 Vigée Le Brun was touring the north of Italy. Her daughter Julie discovered that although she herself was not drawn to painting, she loved to write. The two women moved on to Vienna. The previous Archduchess of Austria, Maria Theresa, was Marie Antoinette's mother, so Vigée Le Brun found another warm welcome. She needed it; the year 1793 was difficult for her. The Reign of Terror was at its height. On June 21 King Louis XVI went to the guillotine; on October 16, Marie Antoinette followed. Jean-Baptiste and Vigée Le Brun's brother Etienne were imprisoned. Their friend David had lost either the ability or the will to shield them.

The Artist at Her Easel.

Vigée Le Brun always secretly hoped to return to her home. Now that seemed impossible. The life she led—as a single woman traipsing from one foreign country to another in search of clients, relying on her skills alone to keep herself and her daughter afloat—now seemed likely to be her life forever.

Her husband Jean-Baptiste also decided he had to separate himself from her to protect his own life and property. His business as an art dealer had evaporated. From prison, he sought a divorce. On June 3, 1794 it became official. Elisabeth was not unaffected. While Jean-Baptiste had been a disappointment, he was also an important connection to her former life. Offsetting this blow was the release of both Jean-Baptiste and her brother Etienne from jail. A public backlash against the Reign of Terror had finally brought it to an end.

Despite her success in Vienna, Vigée Le Brun soon left for Russia. Here, her Viennese friends assured her, aristocrats with deep pockets would be eager to have her paint their portraits. The opportunity to see a new part of the world also appealed. In St. Petersburg in 1795 Vigée Le Brun found a warm welcome from Catherine the Great, who already had a copy of her early portrait of Marie Antoinette. The Academy of Fine Arts elected her a member. In Russia, Vigée Le Brun made a handsome income from painting, but she also lost a lot of money when thieves broke into her house and her bank failed.

Julie, now seventeen, insisted on marrying Gaétan Bernard Nigris, secretary to the director of St. Petersburg's Imperial Theater. Her mother did not like him; she felt Nigris was unreliable. To her, he was "a man with neither talent, fortune, nor family." Vigée Le Brun tried hard to dissuade Julie, but the marriage went forward. The relationship of mother and daughter, never strong, only worsened: "I could not find the same pleasure in loving my daughter, and yet God knows how much I still love her, despite her faults," Vigée Le Brun wrote later in her memoirs.

Back in France the corrective, calmer Directoire (Directory) had come to power. On July 26, 1799, ten years after her flight, Jean-Baptiste presented a petition signed by two hundred fifty-five artists and writers requesting that Vigée Le Brun be allowed to return. The list included not only well-known artists like Fragonard and Houdon, but also, importantly, the still influential David.

Shortly after her marriage, Julie contracted smallpox. Vigée Le Brun nursed her daughter through this near fatal bout. Despite her feelings about Julie's marriage, Vigée Le Brun recalled, "No-one could stop me from running to her bedside. I found her face so swollen that I was only frightened for her sake." After Julie recovered, the artist moved on to Moscow. But finding Moscow's cold unbearable, Vigée Le Brun returned to St. Petersburg. Then, on June 5, officials in Paris finally took her name off the list of banned émigrés. Although it would take a year or so to complete the necessary paperwork, it was now safe for Vigée Le Brun and her daughter to return.

And so they did, arriving at the Rue de Cléry house on January 18, 1802.

The evening of her arrival, her husband and brother arranged a welcome home concert. Vigée Le Brun recalled, "As soon as I entered the room everyone turned toward me; the audience clapped and the musicians tapped their violins with their bows. I was so touched by this flattering welcome that I burst into tears."

Vigée Le Brun had survived twelve years on her own, successfully earning a living as an artist among the highest social circles in Europe, while a wanted woman in her native country. But now, despite their incompatibility, lengthy separation, and divorce, Vigée Le Brun once again took up residence with Jean-Baptiste.

Portrait of Mme. Molé-Reymond.

Elisabeth Vigée Le Brun died on March 29, 1842 at eighty-six, having outlived Jean-Baptiste, Etienne, and even Julie, who died—abandoned by her husband—of pneumonia at thirty-nine.

As biographer Gita May wrote, "Elisabeth Vigée Le Brun presents the unique case of a great woman artist who consistently subscribed to all the political, social, and religious values of Old Regime France, yet was a revolutionary in the way she fearlessly pursued an independent career as a self-taught, self-supporting painter and as an exile wandering on her own in a Europe torn by revolution and war."

Indeed, the young woman who fled her home at midnight to save her daughter and herself in a time of great danger not only succeeded in that goal but also reached the height of her chosen profession, painting her way into history.

Vigée Le Brun is buried in the cemetery of Louveciennes, where she once owned a country house. A palette with paintbrushes decorates her tombstone. She completed over six hundred portraits in her lifetime. They now hang in museums all over the world, including the Louvre itself, where she began her career as just one more eager student in the crowd.

4. ANIMALS EVERYWHERE!

Rosa Bonheur, Painter, France, (1822-1899)

66 I used to spend days and days in slaughterhouses. Oh! You've got to be devoted to art to live in pools of blood, surrounded by butchers," Rosa Bonheur once said.

It's not that the French painter hated animals. Quite the opposite. Bonheur loved them. She visited slaughterhouses to study their anatomy so she could paint them better.

Off she'd go, early in the morning, to the Abbatoir du Roule on the outskirts of Paris. Along the Rue de Miromesnil were several slaughterhouses, long, cavernous buildings with stone floors, lit only by candlelight. The environment was horrific, with hundreds of terrified, bellowing cattle, sheep, pigs, and even horses that had simply grown old. Men in bloody aprons and wooden clogs shouted as they herded the creatures between fences to holding pens where other men killed them with a single blow from a sledgehammer. Removing the

Rosa Bonheur in her studio, by Anna Klumpke.

skin, entrails, and heads, then halving the animals, the men hung the split car-casses on hooks along the wall so butchers from the city could come and pick which to cut into steaks, chops, loins, and ribs to sell to their customers.

Of course there was no way that the twenty-three-year-old Bonheur could bring paints, a palette, and an easel to a slaughterhouse. Instead, she brought a sketchbook and pencil. She drew studies of the animals tied in the pens, wait-ing to die. Somehow Bonheur managed the blood, noise, and chaos all around her.

She also managed to become the greatest animal painter of all time. But how? Bonheur had so much to overcome.

*   *   *

Born Marie-Rosalie in the city of Bordeaux on March 16, 1822, Bonheur grew up in a family struggling to make ends meet. Her father Raymond was a painter and art teacher, but he devoted more of his time to a trendy utopian movement than to providing for his family. The Saint-Simonians, named after their founder, the Count of Saint-Simon, were Christian socialists who dreamed of a less competitive, more cooperative society. War would be obsolete. Men and women would be equal. A female messiah would appear. Developing and discussing these ideas and not, unfortunately, earning a living, was Raymond's focus. Rosa's mother Sophie took up the slack, teaching piano students by day and sewing piecework by night to feed the family.

In 1833, at the age of eleven, Rosa contracted scarlet fever. Sophie nursed her back to health, but then herself collapsed, dying "of exhaustion," as the artist put it later: "I can still see my mother bending down to make me drink my medicine. She'd put her hand on my burning brow, and I'd wrap my arms around her neck and plant long kisses on her beautiful eyes, brimming with tears. Alas! She got so worn out taking care of me that her constitution, already terribly beset by the strain of bearing up so proudly in such wretched circumstances, completely broke down...She died."

Rosa felt the loss for the rest of her life. Luckily, she had a best friend, Nathalie Micas. They grew up to be lifelong companions and lovers. It was characteristic of Rosa that despite her father's and her society's disapproval, she never hid her feelings for Nathalie. A flamboyant personality, Nathalie favored red and black outfits. She loved to wear fancy hats with long plumes. Rosa thought her "a Spanish beauty."

But school was not one of Rosa's strengths. Even learning to read was a challenge. In fact, Rosa succeeded only when her mother asked her to draw a picture of an animal for each letter—a cow (in French, *vache*) next to "V," and so on. Today Rosa might have been diagnosed with dyslexia and received appropriate support. But not in nineteenth century France. Sent to boarding school, Rosa got up one night, snatched up a toy sword, and ran outside. The moon was full; she just couldn't sleep. In the principal's garden, imagining herself as the

Spanish knight Don Quixote from the famous novel of the same name, she cut down the hollyhocks one by one—her enemies! The next morning the furious head of school packed her off, calling her a "dirty little brat."

Rosa was just thirteen. There was nothing her father could see to do but make her his apprentice. Rosa's sisters Juliette, Auguste, and Isidore already worked for him. Eventually all four girls became animal artists, or as the French

Rosa Bonheur with her Favorite Bull, painted by E. L. Dubufe.

called them, *animaliers*. Soon Rosa was copying plaster casts of sculptures and Old Master paintings in the famous Louvre Museum in Paris, learning the trade of an artist. Short in stature, with surprisingly petite hands and feet, nonetheless she had a strong, solid body. Fine brown hair, cut short, topped a broad forehead above large, animated eyes and full lips.

By this time Rosa was already keeping animals in the family's apartment—not only finches, canaries, quails, chickens, and ducks, but also rabbits and even a goat.

This collection would turn out to be just the beginning for Rosa, who was already comfortable with living differently. This included maintaining her relationship with Nathalie.

For a French artist in those days the road to success led through the Salon, the annual exhibition mounted by the national Académie des Beaux-Arts (Academy of Fine Arts) in Paris. Artists submitted their paintings or sculptures and hoped against hope that officials would choose their works. Then people would see and maybe even buy them. Since there were no private art galleries, as there are today, there was no other way to make a living as an artist.

The Salon accepted not just one, but two, of Rosa's paintings in 1841, when she was just nineteen: *Two Rabbits Nibbling Carrots* and *Goats and Sheep*. Rosa not only got into the exhibition, she sold the second work. Just a few years later, in 1847, the Salon accepted eight of her works. Officials awarded her a valuable and beautiful Sèvres vase, as well as a three thousand franc commission to make a large painting with a "plowing motif." Country scenes were fashionable.

Bonheur began work on the new painting right away but was interrupted by her father's death on March 23, 1849. By this time he was head of a small art school for girls, and the painter, now twenty-seven, took it over. The school provided a steady income. Bonheur's pupils loved her. They all cut their hair short to look just like their principal.

Plowing in the Nivernais, completed in 1849, is one of Bonheur's most famous paintings. The Nivernais is a rural province. Bonheur's painting shows two teams of six huge oxen pulling plows through a field. The foreground is so shallow, the first team seems to come right at us as a farmer with a switch drives the powerful beasts forward. Visible behind them is the second team of oxen and a hillside. Bright sunlight falls on the animals, highlighting their powerful muscles, emphasizing and dignifying their labor. The people are far smaller and less important. "Getting down to work" on the painting, Bonheur is reported to have said, she was thinking of more than just the animals: "I also

Plowing in the Nivernais.

had in mind to celebrate the ploughman's art of opening those furrows from whence comes the world's bread." The painting won a First Medal in the Salon that year. Bonheur was surprised, thrilled, and honored when the Museum of Luxembourg in Paris bought it for its permanent collection.

With this success Rosa Bonheur and Nathalie Micas set out on what was to be the first of many trips to the Pyrenees, the rugged mountain range separating France and Spain. They saw wheeling eagles and visited remote villages. Here they were excited to meet cross-border smugglers, the local celebrities. By this time they were living openly as a couple, Bonheur having refused several marriage proposals. "As far as males go, I only like the bulls I paint," Bonheur once remarked. Their relationship fit the two women, if not their era. Bonheur said of Micas, "What would my life have been without her love and devotion! Had I been a man, I would have married her.... I would have had a family, with my children as heirs, and nobody would have had any right to complain." People did, including members of the artist's own family, but that did not dissuade either woman. Bonheur fought both to be an artist and to express her love as she saw fit.

Plowing in the Nivernais was followed by another grand painting, *The Horse Fair*, shown at the 1853 Salon, when Rosa was thirty-one. Eight feet high by sixteen feet wide, and now hanging in the Metropolitan Museum of Art in New York City, Bonheur's picture is considered her finest work. For over a year she had visited the horse market on the Boulevard de l'Hôpital in Paris twice a week just to sketch. A Bonheur expert writes, "At a time when a respectable lady would not even dare venture out unchaperoned into the streets of Paris, Rosa Bonheur spent day after day sketching in horse fairs and slaughterhouses, all crude, insalubrious places in which few women and certainly no ladies would ordinarily dream of setting their dainty feet. Rosa Bonheur did just that, and often alone." And she often dressed like a man, for, Bonheur said, practical reasons. "I was passionate about horses; and what better place to study them than at horse fairs, mingling with all the traders? Women's clothes were quite simply always in the way...." Bonheur wore a long coat or smock, baggy trousers, and boots. To wear them she had had to get a special permit from the Paris police. To persuade them, she produced a note from her doctor stating that she needed the clothes "for health reasons." Bonheur sometimes wore a floppy felt hat to hide her face. Sometimes she carried a pistol. "My skirts would have been a great hindrance," Bonheur noted, "making me conspicuous and perhaps calling forth unpleasant remarks." Her bold, gregarious personality was an asset in this respect. She made male friends easily. In one slaughterhouse Emil Gravel, a tall, brawny forty year-old scalder, warned the butcher boys to lay off taunting her. He roared, "I am this girl's protector, and don't you forget it!"

At home or at social occasions Bonheur happily wore dresses. But she also rode a horse like a man, her legs astride the horse's back, not sidesaddle.

Like *Plowing in the Nivernais, The Horse Fair* has virtually no foreground. Once again we viewers are right up close as handlers parade a circle of rearing, powerful Percherons past us. Like the potential buyers standing to one side, we can't help but admire the horses' power, strength, and beauty. As the men try to control the surging horses, they look like the men in an ancient Greek relief of a similar procession on the famous Parthenon temple in Athens. This work had in fact inspired Bonheur. "I would happen to think about the Parthenon friezes

The Horse Fair.

in a crowd of horse traders trying out their beasts. 'And why not do something like that?' I asked myself." In both scenes it is all the humans can do to manage the straining, rearing animals. The largest animal painting in the world, *The Horse Fair,* as described by a contemporary, "was wildly successful, and the jury unanimously declared that from then on anything [Bonheur] sent to the Salon would be automatically accepted."

In 1853 Bonheur and Micas moved to larger accommodations at 32 Rue d'Assas, where they had a roomy studio and a garden as well as stables and pens for their ever-growing menagerie. This included an otter that kept escaping his tank and climbing into their bed.

An important art dealer, Ernest Gambart, bought *The Horse Fair*, planning to exhibit it in England at a fee of one shilling per viewer. When he invited the artist to accompany the painting across the Channel, Bonheur accepted. Overnight she became an international celebrity. Queen Victoria herself insisted on a private showing and meeting. Bonheur also met Edwin Landseer, the famous English animal painter and one of her heroes, who specialized in dogs. Of course Micas came along. The two traveled through Scotland as well as England, delighting in all the different kinds of farm animals, many of which they had never seen. Bonheur became just as popular in Britain as she already was in France. When Gambart had prints made of her works so the average person could afford to buy reproductions of her paintings, the sales made the artist rich.

Returning to France, Bonheur and Micas moved again, in 1859, to a château in By, on the edge of the 40,000-acre Forest of Fontainebleau. Bonheur was thirty-seven. The complex boasted extensive grounds. There was room for even more, and larger, animals. For animals were not just Bonheur's subjects, they were her life. Soon she and Micas were keeping not only dogs, horses, donkeys, oxen, sheep, and goats, but also red deer, roe deer, izards (goat-antelopes), *mouflons* (wild sheep), boars, monkeys, gazelles, elk, and even a yak, as well as four of "the sweetest and the fiercest lions." These big cats had the run of the estate. Her favorite lioness, Pierette, would stand with her paws on Bonheur's shoulders as they stared into each other's eyes. The artist is said to have re-marked, "If we don't always understand animals, they always understand us." The painter was convinced animals had souls. I know they can love, she said.

Although Bonheur now led a more private life, she kept painting. In 1865 Empress Eugénie, ruling France with her husband Napoleon III, surprised the forty-three- year-old artist with an unannounced visit to By. Here she awarded Bonheur the Cross of the Legion of Honor. Bonheur was the first female artist so recognized. Some years later, officials elevated her to Officer of the Legion of Honor.

Happy years for the two women came to an end on June 22, 1889 when Nathalie Micas died. Bonheur was devastated. A friend, Princess Stirbey, ob-served, "Rosa Bonheur could never have remained the celebrated artist she

Wild Cat.

was without someone beside her, at each instant, to spare her the material cares of the household, the daily worries of existence, and to help her also with moral and physical support, as well as with advice in many things relating to her art. Nathalie made herself small, ungrudgingly, so that Rosa might become greater." Bonheur entombed her partner's remains in the famous Père Lachaise cemetery in Paris, planning to join her there when she died.

However, surprisingly, when a thirty-three year-old American artist, Anna Klumpke, came to By to paint Bonheur's portrait, the animal artist fell in love with her. She invited Klumpke to stay, and she did. Eventually Klumpke wrote what she called an "autobiography" of Bonheur. Of course it couldn't really be an autobiography, because the artist hadn't written it. Nonetheless Klumpke liberally quoted Bonheur, reporting that the painter sometimes referred to Klumpke as "my wife," but also said, "Anna, if you ever fall in love with a man and want to marry, you're always free to leave. I'd be very sad without you, but I only want you to be happy."

When "Buffalo Bill" Cody and his famous Wild West Show visited Paris from the U.S., Bonheur was thrilled. She made many drawings and paintings of the Native Americans who accompanied the colonel, dressed in beaded buckskin. The buffaloes he brought along also fascinated her. Bonheur's glamorous "official" portrait of Cody on a white horse is still the most popular image of him.

Rosa Bonheur died on May 25, 1899 at seventy-seven, after a bout of pneumonia. As the artist wished, she was buried in Père Lachaise next to Nathalie Micas. By Bonheur's direction the statement "Friendship is a Divine Affection" was carved on their gravestone. Klumpke reported the painter once said, "My whole life has been devoted to improving my work and keeping alive the Creator's spark in my soul. Each of us has a spark, and we've all got to account for what we do with it."

Bonheur certainly fanned her spark into the brightest flame. She lived a life ahead of her time as a woman and a lover. A dynamic, world-famous painter who elevated animals to new levels of respect that continue to influence how we feel about them today, Bonheur once said, "I have no patience for women who ask permission to think. Let women establish their claims by great and good works and not by convention."

Portraits of Rocky Bear and Red Shirt, of the Wild West Show.

5. THE UNKNOWN IMPRESSIONIST

Berthe Morisot, Painter, France (1841-1895)

Berthe Morisot stood in a corner of the big room and tried not to show she was trembling. What they were doing was so risky. In Paris in 1874 if painters wanted to make it as artists they had to get their pictures accepted for the annual exhibition of the Académie des Beaux-Arts (Academy of Fine Arts), called the Salon. But thirty-three year-old Morisot and her group of friends didn't paint what the Academy wanted. It liked pictures of great moments in French history, like Napoleon crossing the Alps, or Greek myths, like Zeus visiting Leda.

Morisot and her friends championed a different, fresher style, with bright colors and lively brushstrokes. They didn't paint in studios with models and props, but outdoors, *en plein air* (in the open air). They didn't show heroes and heroines or god and goddesses, but everyday people doing everyday things: women picking flowers in poppy fields, workers picnicking on riverbanks, children playing on beaches, boaters rowing on lakes. Often the sun was shining in their pictures, allowing the artists to feature intense, exciting colors.

So Morisot and her friends were holding their own exhibition, this very spring morning, April 15. In a huge empty photography studio on the second floor of 35 Boulevard des Capucines, quite a busy street. Would anyone come? If so, would they like the paintings? Would they buy? If painters got into the Salon, people bought their work. It had already been "approved." An artist could make a living. Now, Morisot and her friends didn't know what would happen.

Slight, slender, and soft-spoken, Morisot had pale skin, very

Berthe Morisot, painted by Édouard Manet.

dark hair, flashing eyes, classically pretty features, and always a serious expression. She had nine works in the exhibition: three watercolors, two pastels, and four oil paintings: *The Harbor at Cherbourg, Reading, Hide and Seek,* and *The Cradle.* Among the exhibitors, Morisot was the only woman. Monet, Degas, Pissarro, Cezanne, Renoir, and the other men in the group thought so highly of her work they had begged her to join them.

The man at the door called, "*Ouvert!* Open!" and threw back the doors. In swept the very first visitors, the women's ankle-length dresses rustling across the floor, the men in striped trousers and long jackets doffing top hats. Morisot took a deep breath.

Morisot's painting of her daughter Julie reading.

Morisot's former painting teacher, Joseph-Benoit Guichard, came to see. He wrote to the artist's mother, "When I entered, dear Madam, and saw your daughter's works in this pernicious milieu, my heart sank. I said to myself: 'One does not associate with madmen except at some peril....' All of these people are more or less touched in the head. If Mlle. Berthe must do something violent, she should, rather than burn everything she has done so far, pour some petrol on the new tendencies... she must absolutely break with this new school, this so-called school of the future...."

Indeed, the new and different paintings shocked more than a few people. Louis Leroy, a critic for *Le Charivari*, a satirical newspaper, singled out a Monet painting called *Impression, Sunrise*. The scene shows Le Havre harbor at dawn. The sun is a fiery orange disk shimmering through blue and gray morning mists. Leroy wrote mockingly: "Wallpaper in its embryonic state is more finished than that seascape! Impression—I was certain of it. I was just telling myself that, since I was impressed, there had to be some impression in it...." The word stuck. Forever after, Morisot and her group were known as Impressionists. Today the name is not a slander but a compliment.

* * *

Berthe Morisot was born on January 14, 1841 in the central city of Bourges, where her father was a government prefect. Of her three siblings Berthe was closest to her older sister Edmé, with whom she drew and painted from an early age. The two girls were clearly talented, so when the family moved to Paris, the Morisots engaged Geoffrey-Alphonse Chocarne, a Neoclassical artist, to instruct them. However, Berthe and Edmé found his lessons tedious. Discipline, discipline, discipline! So in 1858, when Berthe was seventeen and Edmé nineteen, their parents replaced him with Joseph-Benoit Guichard, a livelier man. He inspired the girls.

Talented enough to attend the prestigious École des Beaux-Arts (School of Fine Arts) in Paris, Berthe and Edmé could not be admitted because they were girls. So after three years with Guichard, they went off to study with a very well-regarded artist, Jean-Baptiste-Camille Corot. The master of the so-called Barbizon School of painters, he and his group were among the first to work outdoors.

Corot urged Morisot, now twenty, to join them in this practice. This way, he felt, she could forge the closest connection to the world she was trying to paint. In the open air she was literally standing in the scene she was painting, smelling, hearing, touching, and breathing it. She could show light, nature, and people as they struck her in the moment, not as she might struggle to recall them later in a studio. Morisot took readily to this fresh, immediate style and the freedom it gave her to choose subjects of her own, from her own life. Using the new approach indoors as well as out, she painted her mother resting on a sofa, her sister checking on her sleeping infant, a maid clearing a dining room. In Morisot's view the daily life and work and feelings of women were as important as any old Greek god or French general in a typical Salon painting.

Five years later, in 1868, Morisot was at the Louvre one day, copying a painting (a common exercise for an art student) when the well-known painter Édouard Manet stopped to observe her. Impressed by her obvious talent, he invited Berthe and also Edmé to his Thursday evening soirées, where he and

A Summer's Day.

his wife Suzanne entertained artists and writers. The Morisot sisters entered a new realm of serious, successful artists—just what they aspired to be. "I think he has a decidedly charming temperament," Morisot said of Manet.

The older man took a close interest in Morisot's development. He urged her to try even bolder, freer brushstrokes. He gave her specific suggestions on how to improve this painting and that, sometimes picking up a brush himself to show her what he meant. One day in 1870 Manet actually overpainted a double portrait of Edmé and Morisot's mother, just days before it was to appear in an important exhibition. "Once he started, nothing could stop him," wrote Morisot later to her sister. "From the skirt he went to the bust, from the bust to the head, from the head to the background...." Mortified, Morisot withdrew the picture from the show.

Manet's best known paintings of Morisot herself are *The Balcony* and *Repose*. The first, painted the year he met her, shows her in a family group. Seated in the foreground, she leans over the balcony railing, gazing out at us. When the painting was first shown,

Édouard Manet's painting of Morisot resting, *Repose.*

Morisot wrote to Edmé, "It seems the epithet of *femme fatale* has been circulating among the curious."

In *Repose*, which Manet painted three years later when Morisot was thirty, the artist relaxes on a divan in a billowing white dress. Some people thought the painting a little too intimate. Was Manet a little (or a lot) in love with Morisot? He drew or painted her no fewer than eleven times, against only three images of his wife.

In any case, Morisot was only incidentally Manet's model. More importantly, she was a fellow artist and colleague, a superb painter herself. For if Manet influenced Morisot, she affected him as well. She pushed him to paint outdoors. She recommended subjects. She suggested he use brighter colors. As their professional lives intertwined, so did their families. The Manets and Morisots even vacationed together, visiting the Normandy seaside one summer.

In 1872 Morisot painted her most famous work, *The Cradle*, now in the Musée d'Orsay in Paris. The painting shows Edmé looking into a covered crib where her daughter Blanche is sleeping. Edmé's face is full of love. She is contemplating more than an individual: she is looking at the very future of her family, the next generation. It's an important human moment. As art critic Jules-Antoine Castagnary writes, "You cannot find more graceful images handled more deliberately than *The Cradle*... the execution is in complete accord with the idea to be expressed."

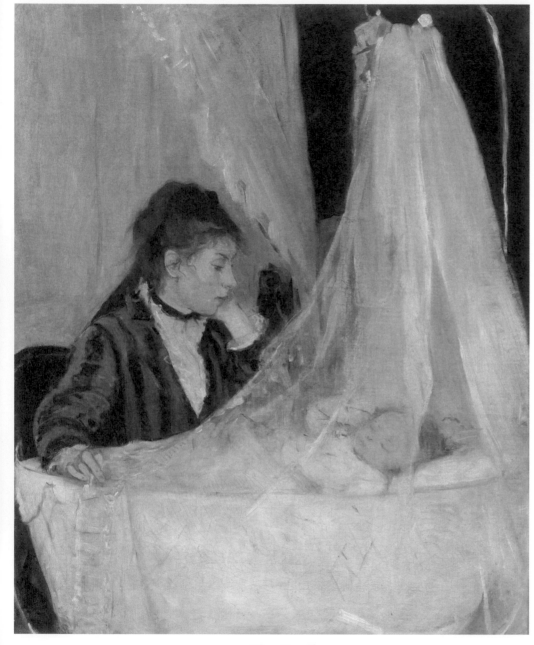

The Cradle.

By now Morisot was regarded highly enough to have her paintings routinely accepted for the Salon, as well as for exhibitions by her Impressionist friends. Furthermore, she sold her work when others did not. Collector Ernest Hoschedé happily bought her 1873 *View of Paris from the Trocadéro*, showing two well-dressed women and a girl outdoors on a grassy prominence overlooking the city. The prestigious art dealer Paul Durand-Ruel agreed to represent her, showing her work in London as well as Paris.

In the fall of 1874, Morisot, age thirty-three, accepted a marriage proposal from Édouard's younger brother, Eugène, wedding him on December 22. A quiet, shy man, Eugène never actually worked at a profession but was a devoted husband. Morisot clearly loved him. When she considered marrying Eugène, she wrote to her own brother, Tiburce, "I have found an honest and excellent man, who I think loves me sincerely." She was correct on all counts.

On November 14, 1878, at thirty-seven, Morisot gave birth to a daughter. Morisot adored Julie from the start, sketching and painting her from infancy through young adulthood. In the paintings Julie plays with a toy boat, walks in the garden with her father, picnics in the country, examines a flower, boats on a pond, pets a greyhound, and plays a violin.

Morisot's subject matter emphasized sunny gardens, light-filled houses, and the pensive, serious girls and women inhabiting them. As an accomplished, recognized artist paying attention to these "ordinary" scenes, Morisot raised girls, women, and their daily activities to a new level of appreciation and respect. Through her many stunning images, she is clearly the outstanding painter of European women in her century.

As Morisot matured, her style grew ever looser and bolder. Colors glowed brighter. An example is *The Cherry Tree*, a breezy summer scene of two girls in

Julie Manet and her father.

an orchard, one high on a ladder, the other reaching up with a basket, brushed in with sweeping strokes of pink, lemon, and ivory. Her courage to move away from the past and investigate the future is a core reason to appreciate Morisot.

The painter led as rich a family life as she did an artist's. When her brother-in-law the famous painter died, on April 30, 1883, she wrote to Edmé, "These last days were very painful; poor Édouard suffered atrociously. His agony was horrible…. If you add to these almost physical emotions my old bonds of friendship with Édouard, an entire past of youth and work suddenly ending, you will understand that I am crushed…. I shall never forget the days of my friendship and intimacy with him…."

Édouard Manet's death made Morisot consider her own career as an artist. Despite all her success, she remained extremely self-critical. Turning forty-nine in 1890, she wrote to Edmé, "I am approaching the end of my life, and yet I am still a mere beginner. I feel myself to be of little account, and this is not an encouraging thought."

When Morisot's husband Eugène, Édouard's brother, died on April 13, 1892, the painter wrote, "I have descended to the depths of suffering… I have spent the last three nights weeping. Pity! Pity!" Morisot was fifty-one. The couple's daughter Julie, who had adored him, wrote, "Often when I dream about Papa, I feel so unhappy when I wake up. I really need him. I want to see him, to hear him, to speak to him, and be nice to him."

In January of 1895 Julie, age sixteen, fell ill with what Morisot called the "grippe," an old-fashioned word for what we call the flu. Morisot did everything she could, of course, to nurse Julie back to health. Julie recovered, but her mother contracted a similar illness herself, which became complicated with pneumonia. Her lungs congested, Morisot was unable to speak or breathe. On the night of March 1, she wrote a last message to her daughter: "My little Julie, I love you as I die; I shall still love you even when I am dead; I beg you not to cry, this parting was inevitable.... Work and be good as you have always been; you have not caused me one sorrow in your little life." Morisot died early the next morning, March 2, 1895 at fifty-four. Julie was a sudden orphan.

Berthe Morisot lived in a remarkable family and prospered there, holding two brothers, sisters, and a daughter in her heart. A hard-working, independent spirit, she completed over a thousand works in oil, watercolor, pastel, chalk, pencil, charcoal and drypoint. She produced lithographs and sculptures. Today Morisot has five works in the Louvre and ten in the Musée d'Orsay. The Tate Museum in London, the Metropolitan Museum of Art in New York, and the National Gallery in Washington prominently display her art. Yet except to scholars, Morisot remains relatively unknown.

This neglect may be receding. In 2013 an art collector bidding in a Christie's auction bought *After Lunch*, painted in 1881 when Morisot was forty, for $10.9 million, then a world record for a female artist.

6. SHAPING A LIFE FROM CLAY

Augusta Savage, Sculptor, USA (1892-1962)

Augusta Savage's wildly popular sculpture group,
Lift Ev'ry Voice and Sing, also called *The Harp*.

No one had seen anything like the 1939 New York City World's Fair. Sixty countries participated with booths and pavilions spread out over one thousand acres just outside the metropolis. At the grand opening on April 30, an unexpectedly hot Sunday, 206,000 people visited, jamming access highways to the Fair. The theme was "the world of tomorrow." Sightseers saw color photography, fluorescent lights, air conditioning, Plexiglas, and robots. "Picture radio" appeared for the very first time. Albert Einstein lectured on cosmic rays. Right in the middle, the gleaming Trylo space needle, soaring 619 feet into the air, was linked by the world's longest escalator to the Perisphere orb beside it, 180 feet in diameter. Together, the structures symbolized an ultra-modern, optimistic future.

In the nearby Contemporary Arts courtyard men, women, and children gathered around forty-seven-year-old Augusta Savage's sixteen-foot high sculpture *Lift Ev'ry Voice and Sing*, the surprise hit of the fair. Based on James Weldon Johnson's song, often called "the Black national anthem," the giant harp featured twelve young singers in choir robes as its "strings." The vertical folds of their clothing made them look like Greek columns. Heads thrown back, the sculpted figures opened their mouths in song. With boxy black Kodak Brownie cameras fathers and mothers photographed their own children standing beside the instrument. In place of the foot pedals at the base knelt a larger than life, muscular man holding a sheet of paper with the song's title. Known more

1939 New York World's Fair.

simply as *The Harp*, the sculpture was so popular the Fair made postcards and miniature versions to sell.

Normally, a sculptor would cast a work of such size and significance in bronze. But when Fair officials asked Savage to produce a sculpture reflecting the power and glory of African-American music, they didn't give her enough money for bronze. Savage had to make *The Harp* out of plaster. When she finished, she painted the sculpture dark gray so it would at least look like basalt, a hard, dark stone often used for sculptures.

The day the Fair closed, October 31, 1940, workers with sledgehammers smashed *The Harp* to pieces. Garbage trucks carted the shards off to a landfill. Only photographs survive.

How could this happen? Perhaps even more surprising, how could a poor girl from rural Florida become a famous artist? Then, soon after, how could she be forgotten, dying in the same poverty in which she grew up?

*   *   *

Born in Green Cove Springs, Florida on February 29, 1892, Augusta Fells was the seventh of fourteen children. From an early age she loved making figures and animals out of the clay she dug from a nearby pit. But Augusta's father was a strict Methodist minister. Because the second of The Bible's Ten Commandments said, "You shall not make for yourself a carved image, or any likeness of anything that is in heaven above, or that is on the earth beneath, or that is in the water under the earth," he forbade the girl to continue. In fact, he beat Augusta when he found her sculpting. "My father licked me four or five times a week," Savage recalled, "and almost whipped all the art out of me."

In 1907, however, when Augusta turned fifteen, her world suddenly changed. Her family left the countryside for the city of West Palm Beach. Here she met a young man named John T. Moore. Though young, they married. A year later Augusta bore a daughter, Irene Connie. She was still in school.

Augusta Savage as
a young girl.

One day on a field trip, the horse drawn wagon carrying Augusta and the other students passed a store with the sign "Chase Pottery." Augusta cried out for the driver to stop. Jumping down, she ran inside. Her excitement was so obvious that Mr. Chase, the potter, gave her some clay to take home, for free. Augusta started sculpting again. This time, when she completed an impressive figure of the Virgin Mary, her father saw her talent in a new light. Perhaps her work could promote rather than obstruct belief in God. He allowed Augusta to continue.

Augusta's talent was so apparent that when she graduated from school, the institution immediately hired her as the art teacher. She earned a dollar a day. Grown into a strong, handsome woman, she had high cheekbones, a strong jaw, and a ready smile. Augusta wore her hair short and pulled back. Large, expressive brown eyes seemed to take in the world with special curiosity.

In 1911, when Augusta was just nineteen, her husband John died suddenly. Four years later, Augusta remarried, to James Savage, a carpenter. Although they soon divorced, she kept his name for the rest of her life.

At the 1919 Palm Beach County Fair, a local lawyer and poet named George Currie noticed Savage's work. As secretary of the fair, he saw to it that she had a booth of her own to show off her work. Savage sold $175 worth of her sculptures, a remarkable sum at the time. She also won a $25 prize for, as the local paper put it, "a picture of Secretary Currie so natural you could see the glasses on his nose." Of course, they had it wrong: Savage made a bust, a head and shoulders sculpture, of Currie, not a painting. But the important thing was that Savage had won public recognition.

Encouraged by her sales, Savage left Irene, her daughter, with her parents in West Palm Beach and moved to the bigger city of Jacksonville, where she hoped to win commissions for sculpture portraits from prominent African-Americans living there. However, there wasn't enough work for the twenty-five-year-old to make a real living. Accordingly, Savage enrolled in the Florida Agricultural and Mechanical College for Negroes, now Florida A & M, in Tallahassee.

But after only a year there Currie, still her biggest supporter, got her admitted to the Cooper Union in New York City, a famous art school which offered scholarships to promising students. Unusually for its time, the school was open to men and women of all races. Cooper Union officials were so impressed with what they saw of Savage's work that they admitted her the day after she applied, ahead of one hundred forty-two other, male applicants. Savage arrived with just $4.60 to her name. The year was 1921, the start of the decade known as the Roaring Twenties. For thirty-year-old Savage, tuition at the Cooper Union was free, but she had to take a job cleaning homes to pay her living costs. She found a small studio apartment in Harlem, the Manhattan neighborhood where most African-Americans were settling.

Then Savage lost her cleaning job. A sympathetic librarian at Cooper Union heard what happened, and he spoke to administrators. They thought so highly of their student that they agreed to underwrite her room and board, as well as her tuition. Another librarian, Sadie Peterson, at the Harlem branch of the New York Public Library, commissioned Savage to make a bust of W.E.B. DuBois, the famous activist, historian, and author.

In 1923 Savage won a summer scholarship to study art in France. It would have been her first opportunity to travel outside the country and see famous sculptures from the past. But when two white women from Alabama who had also won scholarships discovered she was black, they complained about traveling with a "colored girl." The administrators of the scholarships withdrew Savage's offer.

Savage wrote angry protest letters to all of the important New York newspapers.

Savage with her sculpture group, *Realization*.

To the *New York World* she said, "Democracy is a strange thing. My brother was good enough to be accepted in one of the regiments that saw service during the war [First World War], but it seems his sister is not good enough to be a guest of the country for which he fought." Savage's case received widespread public sympathy, but the program's officials wouldn't change their decision.

After the Du Bois bust, Savage won a commission to make a portrait of another powerful and well-known activist, Marcus Garvey, founder of the Universal Negro Improvement Association and the Black Star Line. Through Garvey, Savage met Robert L. Poston, whom she married in October, 1923, when she was thirty-one. Graduating from Cooper Union in only three years instead of the usual four, Savage had little time to enjoy this success or her marriage, however. Garvey sent Poston off to represent him in Liberia, Africa, and on the return trip, in February of 1924, Poston contracted pneumonia and died at sea, before he could even get home. He and Savage hadn't been married for even half a year.

The artist hardly had time to mourn. A hurricane leveled her parents' house in West Palm Beach, and a stroke paralyzed her father, so the family packed up and came to New York to live in Savage's small apartment on West 137th Street. Savage took a job in a commercial steam laundry to support them all, working long hours in crowded conditions over tubs of boiling water and ironing boards piled with dirty sheets and clothes. Having lost three husbands, Savage never married again.

What about her art? No matter what, she was not going to give up that. So Savage turned her tiny basement into a studio, lit from narrow windows at street level.

The painter Norman Lewis noticed. "I discovered her when I was about 23 or 24. We lived on 143rd Street between Lenox [Avenue] and Seventh and I used to walk by her and I looked in the basement and I saw this woman doing sculpture. And it fascinated me, just her ability to manipulate the clay with her hands, clay. And one day I got up enough guts to go into the basement and tell her that I was interested and I would like to learn. She was very open and she let me work in her shop and I started as a sculptor...." Without really meaning to, Savage restarted her career as an arts educator.

In 1925 Savage, now thirty-three, got a second chance to study abroad when DuBois helped her win a scholarship to the prestigious Royal Academy of Fine Arts in Rome. But once again, she couldn't go. Her family needed the money she made from her laundry job.

Savage working up a *maquette*, or small model, of an antelope.

In 1929 a bust Savage made of her nephew, Ellis Ford, age eight, once again brought special attention from the public. Titled *Gamin*, a French word for "street urchin," the lively portrait of Ellis with tilted head, sideways gaze, and floppy hat appeared on the June cover of the distinguished *Opportunity* magazine. In the words of one art critic, the work "effectively captured the essence of her subject's personality: wearing a 'be-bop' cap with its wide brim cocked jauntily to the side, the figure tilts his head in the same direction and looks past the observer with a slightly sullen expression of typical boyhood defiance." One of the few of Savage's works that still exist, *Gamin* may be seen in the Smithsonian American Art Museum in Washington, D.C.

That same year Savage, now thirty-seven, got a third chance to go abroad. The Julius Rosenwald Fund awarded her an $1,800 scholarship to study in Paris. This time Savage could, and did, finally go. When the Fund awarded her a second grant, she went

Gamin, now in the Smithsonian Museum in Washington, D. C..

overseas again. Then the Carnegie Foundation sent her to Belgium and Germany, where she studied sculpture in churches, museums, and palaces. Returning from this tour in 1932, Savage felt she was a much better artist. However, she found commissions hard to come by. Because of the Great Depression, no one had money to spare.

So Savage opened her basement studio to paying students. Jacob Lawrence, later a famous painter, recalled, "And that's when I first met her, but it didn't mean very much to me at that time, you see, because I was about fifteen. I didn't know who she was, I didn't know of her importance in American art. Of course later I did know. She was very influential a few years later in making me a professional really in that she liked my work.... countrywide she was known throughout the Negro communities and probably throughout the American communities when you spoke of the Negro artists... Augusta was one of the big names." Savage didn't completely stop working at her own sculptures. She fashioned busts of the great orator Frederick Douglass and of W. C. Handy, the cornet player and songwriter known as "The Father of the Blues."

In 1934, when Savage was forty-two, the National Association of Women Painters and Sculptors elected her its first African-American member. The U. S. government appointed her to head a federal arts project designed to provide employment for artists hard hit by the Depression. She also expanded her school, naming it the Savage Studio of Arts and Crafts. The school continued to grow. On December 20, 1937 it opened in new facilities as the Harlem Community Art Center, with over a thousand students. First Lady Eleanor Roosevelt herself attended the dedication ceremony.

The year 1939, marked by the great success of *The Harp* at the World's Fair, was also one of disappointment for the forty-seven year-old Savage. Because she had no place to store *The Harp* and no money to cast it, fair workers destroyed it. Expecting to return after the fair to the Center she had founded, Savage discovered she had been replaced. So she opened a small art gallery, calling it the Salon of Contemporary Negro Art. The first gallery in the city featuring African-American artists, it found few buyers and soon closed. Tiny Argent Galleries gave her a one-woman show, but when that ended with disappointing sales, Savage simply stopped making art.

In 1945, at fifty-three, the sculptor moved out of Harlem to the village of Saugerties in the Catskill Mountains, a hundred miles northwest of Manhattan. Here she lived in a house without electricity or running water. She grew vegetables, raised chickens, and put up preserves. She worked on the mushroom farm of K-B Products and in its cancer research laboratory caring for mice. Savage wrote children's books and murder mysteries, but no publishers wanted them. Only in the summer did she occasionally return to sculpture, as a teacher in youth camps or when a tourist commissioned a portrait of herself, himself, or a family member.

A neighbor, Audrey, remembers, "She was very, very poor. She had a rattle-trap car. Her lane was full of ruts and potholes. She would be rattling down the main road in an old Pontiac.... It was the color gray. She carted everything in it like a truck.... She once told me she wished she had named herself 'Helen Augusta Wind' instead of Augusta Savage."

Savage lived in Saugerties for seventeen years. In 1962, sick with cancer, she moved back to Harlem to be with her daughter Irene and her family. There Savage died on March 26 at the age of seventy.

Today, a YouTube video shows her working on sculptures of an antelope and the head of a young man. In Saugerties there is now an Augusta Savage Road. The Augusta Savage House and Studio, where she lived, is listed in the National Register of Historic Places. A high school named for Augusta Savage opened in 2004 in Baltimore, graduating its first class in 2007. In West Palm Beach there is a movement to cast *The Harp* in bronze. If it succeeds, Savage may finally get the attention she deserves.

Otherwise, photographs are the only evidence we have of most of Augusta Savage's works, such as the happy *Laughing Boy*, the proud *Pugilist*, the somber couple of *Realization*, and the exultant, windswept woman of *La Citadelle Freedom*. The actual sculptures, a great legacy, have been lost.

Speaking of her art students in a magazine interview, Savage said, "I have created nothing really beautiful, really lasting, but if I can inspire one of these youngsters to develop the talent I know they possess, then my monument will be in their work." Augusta Savage clearly influenced many young artists. But the first part of what she said to the interviewer is simply not true.

The Augusta Savage Institute of Visual Arts in Baltimore, MD.

7. BETWEEN TWO WORLDS

Pan Yuliang, Painter, China (1895-1977)

In 2003 tens of millions of viewers in China, a country of 1.4 billion people, watched TVB's production *Painting Soul*, based on the life of Chinese painter Pan Yuliang. The well-known actress and model Michelle Reis, a former Miss Chinese International and Miss Hong Kong, played Pan. Never before had any artist, male or female, in any country, been featured at such a scale in any medium. Just one year earlier, in July, 2002, an exhibition of Pan Yuliang's work at the Qingdao Art Museum in the town of Fengcheng drew tens of thousands of visitors, breaking all attendance records. Yet Pan began life as a poverty-stricken orphan. Her uncle sold her into sex slavery when she was thirteen. Even when Pan began to create art, she made paintings that many Chinese hated.

How on earth did she go from being so downtrodden and abused to such fame and respect, leaving a permanent impact on Chinese and international art?

Self-Portrait, 1924.

* * *

Pan Yuliang was born on June 14, 1895 in Yangzhou in Jiangsu province, with the name Chen Yiuqing, into a poor family. Her father died a year after her birth. When the girl's mother died in 1903, a maternal uncle took in the eight-year-old, renaming her Zhang Yuliang with his family name.

Five years later, the uncle sold her to a brothel in the city of Wuhu, Anhui province. Zhang was just thirteen. She had no rights and owned nothing, not even her own body.

While Zhang was in the brothel, revolutionaries in China unseated the Qing dynasty nominally headed by six-year old emperor Puyi. Over two thousand years of imperial rule ended when Puyi abdicated, and on

January 1, 1912 Sun Yat-Sen became president of the new Republic of China. For the rest of the century, China suffered more or less continuous political turmoil over who would govern, including a civil war and a war with Japan. These spasms of history affected the artist's life in many ways, as well as the destinies of millions of other Chinese.

In 1913 a local customs official, Pan Zanhua, who was already married and had a son, took the 18-year-old brothel girl as his second wife or concubine. It was not uncommon for some Chinese men in that era to make such arrangements. Grateful to be out of the brothel, the young woman renamed herself, changing her name from Zhang Yuliang to Pan Yuliang.

In 1916, when Pan turned twenty-one, Pan Zanhua officially married her. He found her an apartment of her own in Shanghai and hired a tutor for her. Pan learned to read and started painting. A neighbor, Hon Ye, an artist and professor at the Shanghai Art School, introduced her to modern Western oil painting, especially the so-called "Fauves" ("wild beasts") from France. These painters used splashes of bright colors to energize their canvases. Color was not as important in traditional Chinese painting, where artists used brushes dipped in black ink to trace graceful lines on paper.

Encouraged by her husband, Pan entered the Shanghai Art School in 1918 at twenty-three, graduating three years later. She was an arresting figure, whose broad face had a large nose, full cheeks, and full lips. Pan wore her thick, dark hair cropped short. She had a deep, husky voice and a strong, direct gaze.

Meanwhile, the early Twenties saw the rise of two opposing political parties in China, the Kuomintang (Nationalist Party) and the Communist Party of China. The Nationalists were led by Chiang Kai-shek, a protégé of Sun Yat-Sen. The Communist leader was Mao Zedong. Throughout the following decades these two groups waged a violent struggle to see which would dominate the country.

Headshot from Pan Yuliang's French identity card, 1921.

After graduating from Shanghai Art School in October of 1921, Pan left for France to further her painting studies, having won a scholarship to study at the Sino-French Institute in Lyon, France. Here she became known for both her talent and her audaciousness. Once, during a three-hour lecture by the head of the school, Wu Zhihui, Pan waved her watch and cried out, "Sir has spoken for too long... please, Sir, rest for a while." He and the other students were outraged, but Pan didn't care.

After two years at the Sino-French Institute, Pan applied to the prestigious École des Beaux Arts in Paris and was admitted. When she graduated in 1925 at thirty, she won a Rome Scholarship to study art in Italy, becoming the first Chinese woman to enroll in the Accademia di Belle Arti (Academy of Fine Arts) in Rome. Once in Italy she won many awards, including a gold medal and 5,000 lira prize at the Italy National Fine Arts Exhibition of 1927.

In 1928 Pan returned to China, where she became active as a painter, teacher, and activist. On October 10, she and other artists founded the Yifan Painting and Research Institute. In November of that year, at thirty-three, she had her first solo exhibition in her native country.

Pan became Chair of the Department of Western Art at Shanghai Art School in 1929, where she had made her start eleven years earlier. In October she mounted a one-woman show in Tokyo. Early the next year, the director of the art department at the National Central University in Nanjing, Xu Beihong, invited her to be a professor.

Despite these successes, Pan suffered severe criticism and animosity from various government officials, jealous male artists, and conservative men. Patriarchal Chinese society was based on a strict hierarchy of social class and gender. Some people resented her origin as a prostitute of the lower class. Plus, she was a woman. Further, Pan painted with Western influences. She also painted nudes, which many of her critics thought improper. Finally, of course, Pan was bold. One of her paintings, *My Family*, shows her seated at an easel, brush in hand. Behind her stand Pan Zanhua and his son, admiring the work she is creating. Some called this scene an affront because Pan was not hiding the fact that she was a "second wife" or concubine. Nonetheless, Pan and sister painter

Guan Zilan became favorites with the general public.

As for the many nudes Pan painted, Eric Lefebvre, a French curator, says, "She used the female body to convey many different ideas, like the ideas of nature, of freedom. She managed to convey a special vision of the woman which is very cohesive with a kind of feminism." Painting single nudes and dance groups in lively colors and poses like those of the French Fauve painter Matisse, her contemporary, she placed them in distinctly Chinese landscapes, mixing together the art looks of both countries. In the past, most pictures of nude women had been painted by men for other men to look at. But not Pan's. Quite the opposite. Says Lefebvre, "This is really her very personal way to express this ideal beauty." In fact, many of her nudes are shown from behind, because Pan felt that featuring the back emphasized the strength of women. Essentially Pan

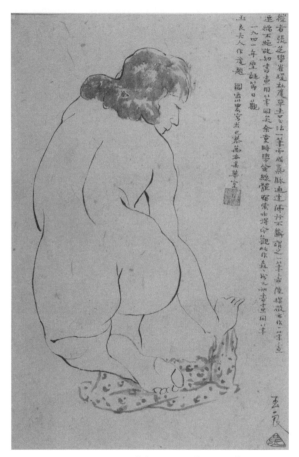

Woman Looking Backwards.

reclaimed the female nude for women. Art critic Phyllis Teo says, "Her recurrent representations of the nude challenged the entire position of the female body in the history of Chinese art and culture."

The Anhui Provincial Museum in China holds the largest collection of Pan's works. In a recent tour of the museum, vice-curator Huang Xiuying explained, "When she was a prostitute, her body was another's tool: there was no soul. But in the artistic world, the body is a respected artwork. It's not hard to understand her complicated and deep feelings for human bodies."

In any case, Pan continued to endure hostility. The story is told that in 1936, during her fifth solo exhibition, "Heroes of Labor," someone tore up one of her paintings on paper. The work showed a man moving a rock to allow a small flower under it to flourish. The man who tore up the painting wrote on one of the pieces, "This is just a prostitute's tribute to her patron."

For Pan, enough was enough. On July 26, 1937, she left China again for France. "Ironically," says Teo, "Pan fled to France specifically because she felt Paris could accommodate a woman's creative energy better than her native country." That same month, a dispute between Japanese and Chinese troops at the Marco Polo bridge near Beijing grew into a full-scale battle. The Japanese overran the Chinese troops, capturing the city. For the next eight years Japan and China fought throughout the land with the Japanese controlling many cities but the Chinese commanding the huge countryside.

Pan Yuliang settled in Montparnasse, a working-class section of Paris where artists lived and congregated because of the inexpensive rents. Artists gathered in the cafés to socialize and exchange ideas about their work. Pan lived in a three-story walk-up attic, which she turned into a studio. It had no running water. She had to carry a jug down three flights and back up again whenever she needed water to drink or bathe.

In Paris Pan experimented further with blending Western and Eastern art styles. She used colored water and ink spots and lines as background, while drawing the figures using oil painting techniques. One critic says of Pan, "By this time in Paris, she had found a way to merge traditional Chinese ink techniques with the adaptations of European modernism to develop a style of her own... She achieved a new way of being modern." Pan outlined subjects in ink, on paper, in the Chinese tradition, but filled them in with bright, modern French colors. For example, in her painting of a cat and five sparrows by a vase of flowers, Pan outlined the cat and birds in ink, while she made the flowers with bursts of vivid pinks, reds, whites, and greens. This was how Pan tried to solve what one critic calls "the dilemma between choosing the influx of modern Western culture and bearing the burden of one's tradition."

If China was suspicious of Pan and her art, France was not. Officials of the three most important annual art shows, the Salons d'Automne, des Indépendents, and du Printemps (Salons of Autumn, the Independents, and Spring), prized Pan's work so highly they allowed her to enter each year without having to pass her works before the selection committees. These shows exhibited the work of "modern" artists like Pan, supplanting the previously more important but very conservative Paris Salon. Pan exhibited in many solo and group shows. She won numerous gold and silver medals in exhibitions across Europe, including the French National Gold Award in 1945, the Belgium Second Prize in 1958, and the Paris Prix d'Or in 1959. The École des Beaux Arts welcomed her as a professor.

Pan predominantly portrayed women. Besides nudes,

Self-Portrait with Flowers.

she painted women who were clothed and performing a variety of activities, such as swimming at the beach, dressing up, bathing children, breast-feeding, laughing together, petting cats, dining out, arranging flowers, and dancing in groups. Pan also painted many women of color. Her 1939 *Black and White in Contrast* showed a black woman and a white woman in an apartment together. Still, the vast majority of the women in her works were Chinese. Pan also produced many self-portraits and still lifes, of flowers, bowls of fruit, and table settings.

Despite Pan's successes, she lived in relative poverty in Paris. If Pan was routinely winning awards for her art, how could this be? Because she left few records, the answer is unclear. There may be several reasons.

First, to sell paintings at that time, an artist had to have her work seen by the buying public. There were only two ways to do this. Showing in the Salons was one way. Pan clearly had access to these shows. A better way was to sign up with an art dealer and show your work in his or her private gallery. More and more artists were doing this. But Pan did not want to be restricted to one gallery, so she never took this path. Although she retained her freedom, she had no predictable place to show and sell her paintings. Her grandson later suggested that Pan lived according to three principles: do not sign contracts with galleries, do not switch to French citizenship, and do not fall in love. Pan prized her independence, even while she suffered from poverty and loneliness.

The advent of World War II also made life hard for artists. Invading France in 1940, the Germans entered Paris on June 14, occupying the city for four long years. Of course the war not only cost lives, but also made everything scarce: food, coal for heat, and clothing. No one had extra money for art. Moreover, the Nazis commandeered Pan's apartment. She had to move out of the city into a suburb, where she taught embroidery, which she had practiced as a teenager in the brothel.

Finally and perhaps most importantly, it seems that Pan was regularly sending money back to China to support her husband Pan Zanhua and his son. Her ties to them were still important to her. The war with Japan continued to disrupt China, and conditions were as difficult and uncertain as they were in France.

On August 25, 1944 the Germans, nearing defeat, evacuated Paris. Pan was forty-nine. For her and the French, World War II was essentially over. Returning to her attic in Montparnasse, Pan developed a relationship with a restaurateur named Wang Shouyi, who also gave her some financial support.

On September 2, 1945, Japan surrendered to the Allies, ending the Second World War. The Japanese surrendered to China on September 9 and began evacuating the country. Now the conflict between the Kuomintang and the Communists exploded. After four more years of armed struggle, on October 1, 1949 the victorious Communist leader Mao Zedong proclaimed the founding of the People's Republic of China. Kuomintang followers retreated to the island of Taiwan.

Pan had hoped to return home, but she did not. At a show of Pan's work in 2017 in Paris, curator Nikita Yingqian Cai, of the Times Museum in Guangzhou, theorized, "She might have had the opportunity to go back to China after the Second World War but something stopped her, which we speculated [was] that she provided the main financial support to Pan Zanhua and his family."

Communist leader Mao Zedong addresses a crowd of supporters.

The 1950s were a time of both challenge and triumph for Pan. She underwent nasal surgery three times. In 1953 she sculpted a bust of the famous educator Maria Montessori on commission. She held a one-woman show at the

Galerie d'Orsay in May. In 1954 she received a letter from Pan Zanhua regretting they had been parted for so long. In 1956 Pan Yuliang applied to the French government to return to China, but officials ruled she could not take her art works with her if she went, so she stayed in France. In 1959 Pan Zanhua died in China. Yuliang didn't hear the news of her husband's death until the next year. When she did, she was devastated that she hadn't seen him one last time.

Invited to the United States in 1963, Pan exhibited her work in one-woman shows in San Francisco (January) and New York City (May), at the prestigious China Institute in America. In June she returned to Paris, where she was in an auto accident in September.

In 1966 Mao Zedong insisted that capitalist and traditional elements of Chinese society were threatening the Communist ideology underpinning the republic. He ordered a so-called "cultural revolution." Under his orders, his government displaced, arrested, imprisoned, and even killed millions of people. It relocated young people from the cities to the countryside to "re-educate" them back to elemental communism, forcing them to work in fields as farmers rather than attend college or pursue a profession. There was no way Pan could safely return home during this time. Her art was far too "Western." Pan's poor health also made the idea of such a long trip dubious, if not downright dangerous. And the French government continued to bar her from taking her art works out of the country.

Only with Mao's death on September 9, 1976 did the Cultural Revolution come to an end. However, it was too late for Pan to return to China. She was now eighty-one, frail, and sick. In a letter to Pan Zanhua's son, she wrote, "I wish I could get my body to recover so I could go back to my homeland," lamenting that she was too weak to travel on an airplane.

Pan Yuliang died on July 22, 1977 in her attic in Montparnasse, at eighty-two.

Pan left no children. Preparing for the end, she had asked her companion Wang Shouyi to bury her in the traditional one-piece Chinese *qipao* and see that her art works were returned to Anhui, because it was the birth province of her

Montparnasse in Pan's day, painted by Frederick Carl Frieseke.

protector. Wang took on both tasks. Pan Yuliang is buried in her *qipao* in Montparnasse Cemetery in Paris with Wang, who died in 1981. A polished black granite headstone bears their names in gold letters.

Pan's art works finally returned to China in 1984. The Anhui Provincial Museum took in 4,749 works: 361 oil paintings, 353 Chinese paintings, 3,982 drawings, thirteen engravings, and four sculptures. Twenty pieces went to the

National Museum of China in Tiananmen Square in Beijing.

Criticized and debased in China during her lifetime, after her death Pan Yuliang was adored and celebrated. In 1988 Fujian Provincial TV Studio produced an eight-part series about her life. In 1994 the Singapore actor Gong Li appeared as Pan in the biopic "Hua Hun" ("A Soul Haunted by Painting").
In July of 2002 huge crowds visited the exhibition of her work at the Qingdao Art Museum, and 2003 saw the TV biography, "Painting Soul." On November 27, 2005, at Christie's Hong Kong auction house, Pan's 1963 oil painting *Artist Self-Portrait* sold for $1.2 million.

Dividing her time between China and France, Pan Yuliang studied, taught, and produced art in both countries. Uniquely, her work balanced Eastern and Western styles, combining the delicate lines of traditional Chinese ink painting with the bold colors of modern Fauvism. The many nudes she painted reclaimed the female body for women.

Today Pan Yuliang is a household name in China. In her art she merged her two favorite countries, as she could not in life.

8. THE SPY THE NAZIS NEVER CAUGHT

Rose Valland, Art Museum Curator, France (1898-1980)

Commemorative statue honoring Rose Valland in Marcq-en-Barœul, France. Picture frames at her feet symbolize art she saved or recovered.

Early on a late July morning in 1944, Rose Valland, a compact, forty-six-year-old woman wearing round glasses and gray hair in a modest bun, climbed the few stone steps to the entrance of the Jeu de Paume art museum in Paris. She was on her way to work. At the top of the steps she presented her *Ausweis*, a brown paper ID pass with her photo, to the Nazi sentry guarding the doorway.

Valland stood silently while the sentry examined the pass. Behind her, she heard the growl of cars and trucks on the big, busy roundabout of the Place de la Concorde at the end of the Champs-Élysées, the broadest boulevard in the city. As she waited, Rose's stomach turned over. She was calm on the outside, always calm on the outside, but inside she trembled with excitement and fear.

Excitement because the Allied armies that had landed in France on June 6, or D-Day, were said to be getting close to Paris. The city, including the Jeu de Paume itself, had been occupied by Nazi soldiers for the last four years. Now the U.S. Third Army under General Patton was moving nearer every day. But there was also fear, because when the Germans left, they might destroy Paris.

As the curator, or caretaker, in charge of the Jeu de Paume, Rose Valland had been working shoulder to shoulder with the Germans every day in the museum. She had to. But she had also been spying on them for four fear-filled years. As a gay woman in 1940s Europe, Rose Valland was not unpracticed in keeping a secret. But lately she thought the Nazis were on to her. She knew they would have her in front of a firing squad within hours if they found her out.

Of course the guard at the entrance knew her well. She came every day, the only French person other than maintenance men allowed inside the famous museum of contemporary art. Before the Germans came to Paris, Jacques Jaujard, Director of all French national museums, had officially appointed Rose Valland head curator of the Jeu de Paume. But the Nazis were really the ones in charge.

Waiting, Valland glanced up at the two pairs of stone columns flanking the doors. Formerly the site of old-fashioned tennis (*jeu de paume*, "palm game"), the long, tall building looked like little more than a giant shoebox of stone. It stood at the west end of the Tuileries Garden, a wide park with gravel paths, flower beds, lines of trees, rows of benches, reflecting pools, and even a small Ferris wheel. At the other end, half a mile away, rose the Louvre, France's greatest and largest art museum. It owned the *Mona Lisa*, the world's most famous painting. Director Jaujard had his office there.

Finally the sentry nodded Valland through. She made her way down the dim first-floor corridor to a small wooden desk in an alcove. On her way she passed hundreds of paintings leaning against the walls of the hall and surrounding galleries, normally used for exhibitions. There were bronze and marble statues, too, as well as antique furniture. The Nazis had turned the Jeu de Paume into a processing center for all the art, jewelry, furniture, and other valuable items they were looting from French museums and Jewish families they had scared off or imprisoned. Every day, gray German army trucks rolled up to the Jeu de Paume, laden with art works.

Valland sat down, relieved to have passed the first trial of her day. She opened a black notebook on the desk before her. It held a list of the art that had come to the museum, from whom it had been taken, and where, in Germany, the Nazis were sending it. As curator, it was Valland's job to keep track of what came in and out. For the Germans. Only for the Germans.

One day Hermann Bunjes, an elite SS officer, had stopped at her desk. A short, thin man with white hair, round glasses, and a sharp nose, he leaned over her, reached out, and slammed her notebook shut. "That is enough!" he commanded. "There is to be no French record." No record of the masterpieces that were coming into the museum and going out, he meant.

In a soft voice, Valland said of course she understood. She explained that her notes were for German eyes alone. But that was not true. Every day Valland secretly memorized the lists she made, then returned to her apartment and wrote them all down in another, secret notebook of her own. Once she knew where a shipment was going, she alerted her contacts in the French Resistance. They could tell the Allies where in Germany not to bomb, so the art would not be destroyed. And if the Allies ever won the war, the French could go and get the art back.

Looking down at her book, Valland reviewed the entries in black ink in her own looping cursive hand. There were the titles of the latest paintings and sculptures the Germans had brought in. The normally quiet museum had become, Rose later recalled, "a strange world... where masterpieces arrived to the sound of boots." Workers bustled back and forth with crated paintings and statues on dollies. German officers passed back and forth in twos and threes. Valland heard German, not French. *Ja*, not *oui*. *Nein*, not *non*.

* * *

Born in 1898 in tiny Saint Étienne de Saint Geoirs to a blacksmith father and a mother who loved and supported her, Rose Antonia Maria Valland was a bright, dutiful pupil. After attending Grenoble Teachers College on a scholarship, she earned the highest score on the entrance exam for art teachers to the national École des Beaux Arts in Paris. A serious, highly motivated student, Rose developed the study habits and ability to memorize that she later used at the Jeu de Paume. After graduating from the École in 1925 at twenty-seven, she attended the University of Paris and studied at the great Louvre museum. Valland steeped herself in French artistic culture until she knew more than almost anybody.

Valland first came to the Jeu de Paume as a volunteer assistant curator. Although she received no pay, she still felt she had the job of her dreams. To look after the four thousand art works in the museum as if they were her own! She considered it a privilege to protect them from sunlight, dampness, rodents, rot, mishandling, thieves, even visitors (don't touch—!), so they would always be there for all of France to enjoy. The art works included some of the most beautiful paintings and sculptures in the world from recent times, such as Monet's sun-splashed fields and Degas' prancing racehorses and graceful bronze "Young Dancer."

Valland studied the art works, mounted exhibits, and wrote articles. She supported herself by teaching drawing at a nearby high school. But when Nazi tanks smashed through the Ardennes Forest into France on May 13, 1940, rolling through farmland and burning houses as they came, Rose Valland's quiet world turned upside down. World War II came to the Jeu de Paume. In July, 1941 the chief curator of the museum, André Dézarrois, fell sick. Jaujard put Valland in charge. Valland knew he would never have given a woman such a responsibility in peacetime. But there was no one else; except for Dézarrois, the male curators had fled for their lives. Luckily, Valland was well prepared, in practice and character, to assume the leadership.

Entrance of the Jeu de Paume museum, where Valland had to present her pass daily.

Now it was four years later, July of 1944. Valland got to her feet. Taking her notebook, she walked to the end of the corridor and descended the stairway to the basement, where even more art was stored. The door to the loading dock was open. Soldiers were packing paintings, statues, tables, and chairs into a truck. One of the French custodians was taking a cigarette break. Valland quietly stepped to his side. She knew he saw and heard even more than she did, down here.

They spoke in French. They knew the Germans couldn't hear them over the dragging of the crates, their own shouts back and forth, the tramp of their boots. Yes, said the custodian, this truck was for the big shipment going out of the country on August first. By train? she asked. Yes, by train. Over the years the Germans had taken out over 20,000 art works by rail. But this was the last trainload, their final opportunity before the Allies showed up. They were making it as substantial as they could. How big? He shrugged. Over a hundred crates from the Jeu de Paume. At the railway station, perhaps five boxcars just for the art. Many more for the furniture.

Valland thanked him and stepped away. Now she had specific information to report to Director Jaujard. She would visit him at lunchtime. The Nazis were launching one last effort, an entire trainload of some of the finest art and household effects. It was possible the Resistance could stop the train before it left Paris.

Valland didn't ask where the train was going. That she would find out later. She knew that in general the best of everything went to Hitler himself, for the grand museum he was planning in Linz, his mother's hometown. The next best went to Hermann Goering, his second in command, head of the Gestapo and Luftwaffe, the air force. Only then did German museums get to choose.

Valland returned to her desk and drew a deep breath. Events were heading to a climax, good or bad. In a way, Valland was glad. She had lived with constant danger for so long. Once she had been at her desk trying to make sense of a scrawled address on a form when suddenly Bruno Lohse, another Nazi official, stopped beside her. He had a narrow face, dark eyes, a bony nose, and slicked-back hair. A former art historian, Lohse wore a business suit, not a uniform. But that didn't make him any less menacing. "What are you doing?" he barked. Hands on hips, he glared over her. "You could be shot for any indiscretion, you know!" He meant, doing anything she hadn't been told to do.

Meeting his stare, Valland beat back the fear rising inside. She calmly replied, "Anyone here would be stupid not to realize the risk he or she is facing."

Lohse walked on. Inside, Valland was shaking. Later she said, "Each day it was the same, and I never got used to it." She knew that if they ever found out what she was doing, they would put her in front of a firing squad, perhaps in the courtyard of the museum itself, down on the sandy ground she could see from her desk. Standing straight in her gray suit, she would be brave. But neither family nor any friend would know what was happening. She would take the bullets in her chest all alone. For art. For France.

Valland knew why Lohse was so menacing. He was afraid. The Nazis were breaking international law. In 1907, European countries meeting at The Hague in the Netherlands drew up a document declaring that in war, "private property cannot be confiscated" (Article 46). Furthermore, Article 56 added: "All seizure of, and destruction, or intentional damage done to such institutions, to historical monuments, works of art or science, is prohibited...." *Seizure of... works of art...is prohibited....* What could be clearer?

A work on the list in Valland's notebook suddenly jumped out at her: *Seated Woman, 1921, by Henri Matisse, from the Paul Rosenberg Gallery, rue de La Boétie, Paris....* If Valland could have viewed it, she would have seen a dark-haired woman in a white blouse, in an armchair, holding a fan, staring confidently out at us. A bright red carpet enlivened the scene.

Valland knew the gallery and its owner, an art dealer. Paul Rosenberg had his showplace at 21 rue de la Boétie. He and his family lived next door. He owned over two thousand art works, including thirty Picassos. Just before the Germans arrived, Rosenberg, his wife, and his daughter fled to Portugal. His son Alexandre escaped to England. The Rosenbergs had to leave behind everything they owned. Four days later, German trucks pulled up to their house and gallery. Soldiers yanked paintings from the walls. They stripped the family's jewelry from bureau drawers. They dragged antique chairs and tables from the living and dining rooms. Then they trucked everything across the city to the Jeu de Paume.

At twelve o'clock Valland stepped out of the museum into the Tuileries Garden. At the other end of the garden stood the huge Louvre museum, where she would meet with Director Jaujard at his office. As Valland strode along the central promenade, the Seine glittered on her right. Pigeons flew up beside her. She felt, for a moment, almost serene. But the truth was that for Valland, every day was fear-filled, every night sleepless. Each evening was a weary two-mile journey to her apartment at 4 rue de Navarre, minimally heated in the winter. Clothing, coffee, meat (really, any kind of food) was hard to come by.

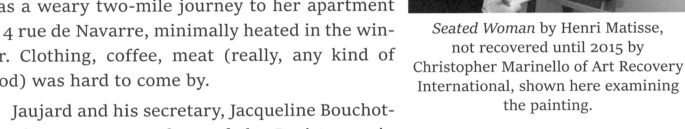

Seated Woman by Henri Matisse, not recovered until 2015 by Christopher Marinello of Art Recovery International, shown here examining the painting.

Jaujard and his secretary, Jacqueline Bouchot-Saupique, were members of the Resistance, in close contact with its fighting arm, the FFI (French Forces of the Interior). Reporting the train and its contents, Valland begged them to do anything they could to delay its departure until the Allies arrived. From a driver she had spoken with, she was able to provide the actual number of the train, No. 4044. Jaujard and Bouchot-Saupique expressed their gratitude. Valland returned to her desk in the little museum at the other end of the Garden with a ray of hope.

Hope was what kept her going. The determination to protect France's art, its national heritage. For French people, art was the soul of their culture. Everyone, even children, knew the *Mona Lisa* and the *Venus de Milo*. Painters and sculptors were culture heroes and heroines: Claude Monet the Impressionist, Berthe Morisot the portrait painter, Auguste Renoir the master of light, Rosa Bonheur the animal artist. They were like Aretha Franklin, Rosa Parks, Cesar Chavez, or Babe Ruth in the U. S. Their works were national treasures. Nazis had killed thousands of French men and women and overrun their land. But if the Nazis thought they were going to steal the art of Rose's country, *her* art, they were sadly mistaken. Yet that is exactly what they were trying to do.

On August 1, trucks carrying one hundred forty-eight crates of art and furniture left the Jeu de Paume for the Aubervilliers railroad station on the other side of Paris. Workers loaded the crates into five boxcars of Train

Outdoor mural in Valland's home town showing her with recovered art works.

4044. The paintings included works by Monet, Cezanne, Matisse, Gauguin, and Picasso, all world famous, and many from the Rosenbergs' own collection.

But the train did not leave immediately. The Germans waited for forty-seven more truckloads of furniture. In the meantime, General Patton's U. S. Third Army and France's 2nd Armored Division were closing in on the city. On August 10, French railroad engineers, emboldened by the proximity of the Allies, went on strike. Train 4044 sat on a siding. For the next two weeks, the only trains departing carried passengers, escaping German soldiers and officials.

A 1964 film, *The Train*, sensationalizes the story of the art shipment. Rose Valland appears briefly as "Mademoiselle Villard." To the male lead, actor Burt Lancaster playing a Resistance fighter, she makes remarks that Rose herself might have made had she been less reticent. Meeting secretly at the rail yards with Lancaster and two other men, she implores them to stop the train: "The Germans

Movie poster for *The Train*, 1964.

want to take everything away. They've taken our land, our food. They live in our homes. And now they are trying to take away our art. Those paintings are part of France. We hold it in trust, don't you see, for everyone, we hold it for all of the world. There are worse things in life to risk your life for than that."

When she leaves, one of the men remarks, "She's a nice lady." Of course, the real Rose Valland was far more than that.

On August 19, around midday, street fighting broke out in Paris between the FFI and the Germans. At the same time the Nazis began a massive retreat of trucks, cars, motorcycles, and other vehicles down the Champs-Élysées and out of the city. A German unit surrounded the Jeu de Paume. Wrapping it with barbed wire and parking their trucks around it, they made the museum part of the line of defense for the luxury hotels in the nearby Rue de Rivoli, where high-ranking Nazi officers stayed. By this time all the Germans working inside the Jeu de Paume were gone. Only Valland and two French custodians remained. It was far too dangerous for Valland to try to get home.

That night Valland, stuck in the museum, didn't sleep at all. The next morning, at 8:00 A.M., she showed herself outside the front entrance to demonstrate to the Germans in the street that the building was not occupied by French troops. They need not attack it. Standing between the columns in the doorway, she casually crossed her arms, hoping to show that there was "just a woman" here. Raising his rifle, a German soldier pointed it straight at her. When he did not lower it, Valland turned and went back indoors. She was trembling inside, but she hoped she'd made her point. And the Germans did not bother the museum.

That afternoon, the FFI attacked the German soldiers outside the Jeu de Paume. From inside the museum, Valland listened to gunshots echoing among the Jeu de Paume and nearby buildings. One young German died on the steps of the museum, where Valland showed her pass every day. The FFI killed eight others before the Germans surrendered. Valland watched her countrymen herd some three hundred fifty prisoners into the Tuileries Garden.

Two days later, Train 4044 finally pulled out of Paris, but it "broke down" almost immediately at Le Bourget, just a few miles out

Liberation of Paris, August 26, 1944.
Cheering crowds line the Avenue des Champs Élysées.

of the city. In fact, members of the Resistance had disabled its locomotive. French mechanics spent two long days "repairing" the engine. Meanwhile the Resistance derailed two other trains, blocking the entire railway system. Before the tracks could be cleared, at 9:22 PM on August 24, the first elements of the 2nd French Armored Division arrived at the Hôtel de Ville in Paris. The next day, the Germans officially surrendered the city.

On August 27, a unit of the 2nd Armored, under Lieutenant Alexandre Rosenberg, who had returned from England to join the fight, captured the art train at gunpoint just outside of Paris at the Aulnay railway yards. In the boxcars he found four hundred items belonging to his own family, including several Matisse paintings, which Rose had duly noted in her records.

French Army Captain Rose Valland.

Yet Valland still wasn't out of danger. Hysterical crowds celebrating the Allied victory swept into the Jeu de Paume looking for Germans they heard were working there. Finding none, they accused Valland of hiding Nazis in the basement. An over-excited Parisian thrust a submachine gun into her back, demanding that Valland take his group downstairs. Valland led them all to the basement. As she wrote later, in understatement, "I was totally relieved that no German soldiers were discovered during this unpleasant expedition."

Valland's work earned her a commission as a captain in the French army. In 1948, three years after the war ended, when she was fifty years old, she was posted to Berlin, Germany, to find and recover as much stolen art as she could. Of course, Valland had the most detailed records of where everything had been sent. She traveled all over, visiting the places where the Nazis had stored what they had stolen, looking for the works in her notebooks. Among the hiding places was the vast Altaussee Salt Mine. Here the Nazis hid over six thousand art works to protect them from being bombed. Valland also found many stolen items at the turreted Neuschwanstein castle in the Bavarian forest, which Disney later copied for its logo. Determined to get back every art work she could, Valland spent three full years in Germany following the

US Army Captain Edith Standen and Rose Valland with art to be returned to France.

clues in her notebooks. She often worked with American curator Edith Standen, another famous name in art recovery.

Valland also met the love of her life, Joyce Helen Heer. A photograph of Heer shows fluffy shoulder-length hair; wide-set eyes; a small, sharp nose; and lips on the verge of a smile. Born in Liverpool, England, Heer was a scholar of ancient Greece. She worked as an interpreter and administrative assistant for the U. S. ambassador in Paris before being briefly imprisoned by the Nazis. Sharing a passion for art, Heer and Valland became companions, then lovers, then partners.

Returning to Paris in 1951, the pair lived together in Valland's apartment while Heer studied for a Ph.D. at the prestigious Sorbonne University and Valland took up official duties as a conservator of the National Museums of Art. In 1958 Valland was named Chair of the Commission for the Protection of Works of Art. In both roles Valland persisted in searching for works others had given up hope of finding. While some colleagues found her insistence annoying, Valland's instincts have been borne out by history. Stolen works are still showing up today, in private and public German collections. Descendants of their pre-war owners continue to mount lawsuits to get them back.

When Heer died of breast cancer in 1977, Valland saw her buried in the family vault in Saint Étienne de Saint Geoirs. Valland also ensured that Heer's doctoral dissertation, *La Personnalité de Pausanias (The Personality of Pausa-*

DE L'AUTOMNE 1940 A L'ETE 1944,
LE BATIMENT DU JEU DE PAUME
FUT REQUISITIONNE PAR LES FORCES D'OCCUPATION
POUR ENTREPOSER, TRIER ET EXPEDIER EN ALLEMAGNE
DES OEUVRES VOLEES A DES COLLECTIONNEURS,
DES MARCHANDS D'ART, DES ARTISTES
ET DE SIMPLES PARTICULIERS DE CONFESSION JUIVE.

SUR L'ORDRE DE JACQUES JAUJARD,
DIRECTEUR DES MUSEES NATIONAUX,

ROSE VALLAND,
ATTACHEE DE CONSERVATION AU MUSEE DU JEU DE PAUME,
SUIVIT ET ENREGISTRA QUOTIDIENNEMENT CES OPERATIONS
A L'INSU DE L'OCCUPANT, MALGRE LES RISQUES ENCOURUS.
CETTE MISSION PERMIT ENSUITE LA LOCALISATION
ET LA RESTITUTION DE PLUS DE 45 000 OEUVRES D'ART.

LA PRESENTE PLAQUE A ETE DEVOILEE LE 27 AVRIL 2005
PAR RENAUD DONNEDIEU DE VABRES,
MINISTRE DE LA CULTURE ET DE LA COMMUNICATION,
EN HOMMAGE A CET ACTE DE COURAGE ET DE RESISTANCE.

Plaque on exterior of Jeu de Paume
commemorating Rose Valland.

nias) was published. Pausanias was an ancient Greek traveler and writer. In the introduction to this book Valland publicly acknowledged her relationship with Heer for the first time.

In 1969 France recognized Valland's efforts nationally, naming her an Officer of the French Legion of Honor and awarding her the Medal of Resistance. Her country also made her a Commander of the Order of Arts and Letters. The U.S. recognized Valland as an honorary Lieutenant Colonel and bestowed on her its Medal of Freedom.

Today a marble plaque with Valland's story decorates the outside of the Jeu de Paume, crediting her with the recovery of over forty-five thousand works of art. A visitor to Saint Étienne de Saint Geoirs will find the middle school named for her. So is the town square, now Place Rose Valland. Recently a mural has appeared on an apartment building, showing Valland in her Army uniform, unpacking a crate of paintings.

Rose Valland died on September 18, 1980, at the age of eighty-two. By her own direction, she was buried beside Joyce Heer. A trove of letters between the two of them, as well as some notes from the war, still unshared, are now the property of heirs. These have yet to be published. Valland was secretive to the end.

The quiet curator is featured in two Hollywood films (*The Train* and the 2014 *The Monuments Men*). However, her real name is never mentioned, and she is presented as a minor character. In real life, she was anything but minor. She not only survived World War II surrounded by deadly enemies every day, she outsmarted them. Daily risking her life for the art of her country, she made sure its heritage survived as well. Rose Valland was the highly effective spy the Nazis never caught.

9. ART OVER PAIN

Frida Kahlo, Painter, Mexico (1907-1954)

On the bright fall day of September 17, 1925, a yellow Mexico City trolley collided full speed with the bus in which Frida Kahlo, age eighteen, was riding home from school with her boyfriend Alejandro. Smashing into the bus from the side, the trolley buckled it in the middle like an empty soda can. The explosion of shattering glass and shredding metal hurled Alejandro into the street, tore off Frida's clothes, and crushed her into a twisted rag doll. All around her people screamed and sobbed. Bleeding bodies lay in contorted positions. As passersby rushed to help, Frida was in such pain she could hardly breathe.

She dislocated her left shoulder and broke two ribs, her collarbone, her spine and pelvis, each in three places, and her right leg in eleven places. As a later medical report noted, she also endured "a penetrating abdominal wound caused by [an] iron handrail entering [her] left hip, exiting through the vagina."

Self-Portrait with Thorn Necklace and Hummingbird.

A man in the bus kneeled down and took hold of the metal bar. Alejandro, watching, recalled, "When he pulled it out, Frida screamed so loud that when the ambulance from the Red Cross arrived, her screaming was louder than the siren.... I picked up Frida and put her in the display window of a billiard room. I took off my coat and put it over her. I thought she was going to die. Two or three people did die at the scene.... others died later."

The first responders didn't believe she was alive. Only because Alejandro wouldn't leave them alone, shouting and screaming at them, did they finally bandage her, lift her into an ambulance, and transport her to a hospital. Even if she lived, what kind of a life could Frida possibly expect?

Born Magdalena Carmen Frieda Kahlo y Calderón on July 6, 1907 at "The Blue House," her family's home in Coyoacán, outside Mexico City, nonetheless Frida Kahlo always gave her birth date as July 6, *1910*, because 1910 was the first year of the Mexican Revolution. An ardent political activist, she wanted to think of herself as "born with the Revolution." She had three sisters: Matilde, Cristina, and Adriana. Her mother Matilde was of mixed Spanish and Indian background. Mother and daughter did not get along. Frida's father, Guillermo, was a German immigrant and enthusiastic amateur painter. They were very close.

As a child Frida contracted the disease of polio, which shriveled her right leg and foot. Early schoolmates teased her unmercifully as "Frida Peg Leg." She said later, "I developed a horrible complex, and to hide my leg I wore thick wool socks up to the knee with bandages underneath." And while Frida supported the Mexican Revolution, when it actually happened, her father, a government photographer, lost his job, plunging the family into poverty. The sisters took after-school jobs. Frida worked as a pharmacy assistant, then a cashier. Later she worked for a printmaker, Fernando Fernández. Copying artists' paintings for Fernández's reproductions was how she learned to draw.

She had no formal art instruction.

In 1922, at fifteen, Frida entered the elite National Preparatory School to study to be a doctor, one of only thirty-five girls among two thousand pupils. There she met Alejandro Gómez Arias and became part of a group of lively students who called themselves *los cachuchas*, after the red caps they wore. They were interested in literature, politics, the Revolution, and each other. It was a very happy time for Frida.

After the 1925 accident, Frida spent two months in the hospital, then another two at home in a full-body plaster cast. Bedridden, she could not of course attend school. Even though friends kindly dropped by from time to time, she was miserable. When Alejandro got an opportunity to study in Europe, he broke up with her and went abroad.

In 1926, a year after the collision, in continuing pain, Frida returned to the hospital. Doctors discovered three vertebrae were still out of place, pressing agonizingly on nerves. For nine months Frida lay immobilized in an upper body cast. Now she couldn't even sit up. Utterly bored, she asked to borrow her father's paints and brushes. Hospital workers hung a mirror over her bed, and Frida painted self-portraits using a special easel her mother made for her. These were the first of many self-portraits she painted in her lifetime. She acknowledged, "I paint myself because I am so often alone and because I am the subject I know best."

Frida continued to paint at home, not just self-portraits but images of her school friends, too. By the end of 1927 she was finally free of the cast. She could move, get around, resume a more or less normal life. A bright spot was meeting the famous Mexican painter Diego Rivera. Rivera specialized in murals of the history of Mexico and the story of the Revolution, executed on a large scale in public buildings where people could see and learn from them. In 1927 he was working on "The Ballad of the Revolution" at the Ministry of Education in Mexico City. When Rivera invited her to show him her work, she took him four paintings to review.

Rivera liked her work—and Frida, too. He became a family friend, visiting often. Forty-one years old and married to Guadalupe Marín, he stood six feet one inch tall and weighed over three hundred pounds. Frida was just twenty, stood five three, and weighed ninety-eight pounds. When Frida's father saw them together, he called them "the elephant and the dove." Rivera had a big, round head and thick hair brushed straight back. He painted Frida into his Mexico City mural.

On August 21, 1929, after Rivera divorced Guadalupe, Kahlo married him. He was forty-three, she twenty-two, just a little more than half his age.

Almost immediately the couple left for the United States, where Diego had commissions. Over the next three years Kahlo and Rivera traveled to San Francisco, Detroit, and New York City, where Rivera painted his trademark murals. They found themselves celebrities: Rivera, for his art; Kahlo, purposely dressing as traditionally "Mexican" as she could, for her look, if not her art.

Kahlo and the muralist Diego Rivera.

To her white cotton *huipil* blouse Kahlo often added the long, brightly colored skirt of the Tehuana women of Southwest Mexico, the shawl or *rebozo* they favored, and even a floral headpiece. The look emphasized her Mexican heritage, so important to her. *Vogue* magazine noted, "From the bright, fuzzy woolen strings that she plaits into her black hair and the color she puts into her cheeks and lips, to her heavy antique Mexican necklaces and her gaily colored Tehuana blouses and skirts, Madame Rivera seems herself a product of her art, and, like all her work, one that is instinctively and calculatingly well composed."

Kahlo was pleased by the attention but ambivalent about the U.S. They were visiting during the Great Depression. The poverty Kahlo saw struck her hard. She wrote to a friend, "Although I am very interested in the industrial and mechanical development of the United States, I find that Americans completely lack sensibility and good taste.... High society here turns me off and I feel a bit of rage against all these rich guys here, since I have seen thousands of people in the most terrible misery without anything to eat and with no place to sleep."

The visit ended badly. On July 4, 1931 Kahlo suffered a painful miscarriage, the second of three in her lifetime. The doctors told her that because of her damaged pelvis she would never have children. Kahlo was also homesick for Mexico. Rivera, on the other hand, was eager to stay in the U.S. Estranged,

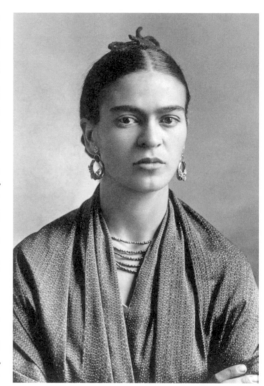

Kahlo in 1932 at age 25, photo by her father Guillermo.

both began affairs, he with sculptor Louise Nevelson, she with photographer Nickolas Muray. Throughout their marriage, this pattern repeated. Letters and reports linked Frida with women, including the actress Dolores del Rio, as well as men. Betrayal, jealousy, and hurt muddied any love Kahlo and Rivera seemed to share.

When the couple finally returned to Mexico in 1933, Kahlo was twenty-six. Rivera began a relationship with her younger sister, Cristina. Frida and Cristina were close, and when Kahlo found out, she was devastated. Leaving Rivera, she took an apartment of her own in Mexico City. She lamented, "I have never loved anyone who loved only me. I have always shared love with another."

But once apart from Rivera, Kahlo blossomed personally and artistically. Her work suddenly attracted attention. The Julien Levy Gallery in New York City gave her an exhibition. She sold four paintings to the Hollywood actor Edward G. Robinson. She traveled to Paris to exhibit her work and met Picasso, who gave her earrings in the shape of hands. The Louvre Museum bought a colorful self-portrait, *The Frame*. This was a huge honor. By now, Kahlo's reputation was eclipsing Rivera's.

The two reconciled for a while, but finally divorced in November of 1939, when Kahlo was thirty-two. She moved back into the Blue House, her childhood home. She gave up the traditional Mexican and Tehuana outfits. A stark self-portrait from this period shows Kahlo in a man's business suit with cropped hair. She holds scissors in her hand. Tufts of hair litter the ground. The message? She is pouring all her energy into art.

In 1940 she painted her famous *Self-Portrait with Thorn Necklace and Hummingbird*. Below jet upswept hair and thick eyebrows, brown eyes fix us with a steady gaze. A small mouth with full, red lips punctuates the face. Mexican folk features such as the dead hummingbird, her pet monkey, and the simple *huipil* help define her. Although the animals and setting are "real," there is an otherworldly feeling, too, in how the monkey and black cat seem so like a witch's familiars. This two-world feeling permeates much of Mexican tradition. On the November "Day of the Dead," for instance, people may picnic in cemeteries with the spirits of their ancestors.

Then Kahlo's back acted up again and she couldn't shake an infection in her right hand. Traveling to San Francisco to consult Dr. Leo Eloesser, she ran into Rivera, who was executing a mural there. Rivera asked Kahlo to marry him again, and she agreed! But when they remarried, on his birthday, December 8, 1940, she insisted on two rules: she would support herself from the sale of her own art, and she would pay only half of the household expenses.

Returning to Mexico, they moved into the Blue House. For Kahlo, now thirty-three, the following years were artistically rewarding. She started her now-famous diary. In 1943 the National School of Painting and Sculpture, just opened in Mexico City, appointed her a professor. However, the pain in Kahlo's back again became terrible. In 1944 doctors operated on her spine once more. Afterward, she had to wear a steel-braced corset. Kahlo could no longer leave the Blue House, although dedicated art students visited her there. A contemporary self-portrait, *Broken Column*, suggests her feelings. The painting shows her naked, facing the viewer, her body split open from head to hips. Inside, where her spine should be, is an ancient Greek column, broken into pieces. Numerous nails in her breasts and flesh symbolize her pain. A few cloth straps are all that hold her together.

Broken Column, symbolizing Kahlo's conception of her condition.

Thankfully, in 1945 Kahlo won a national prize in Mexico for her painting, "Moses." Unlike her other works, this large image is crowded with people. A great solar ball looms over the infant prophet, floating in a basket on a river, while Man and Woman look on, as well as over thirty-five other figures, including Buddha, Queen Nefertiti, Gandhi, Muhammad, Jesus, Napoleon, Hitler, the Virgin Mary, and various Greek and Mexican gods and goddesses.

By the night of her first ever one-woman show in Mexico, in April of 1953, Kahlo was completely bedridden. However, the forty-six year-old artist insisted on attending. Friends and family carried her into the Gallery of Contemporary Art on a stretcher to settle her into her own bed, which they had delivered earlier. Although heavily sedated for her pain, Kahlo was thrilled to see her work finally so esteemed in her native country.

That August, doctors amputated Kahlo's right leg below the knee as gangrene threatened. The artist found it hard to recover psychologically. On July 2, 1954 she insisted on attending an outdoor political protest with Rivera, although at the time she was suffering from pneumonia. Eleven days later Frida Kahlo died, at age forty-seven. The official cause of death was a pulmonary embolism, a blood clot traveling to the lungs. However, Kahlo's niece Isolda later reported that Rivera once admitted to a family member that he had given Kahlo a fatal overdose of her medicine, to free her from "this slow death, this cruel and senseless torture." It is still not clear what really happened.

Rivera himself died three years later, on November 24, 1957.

The Blue House is now the Frida Kahlo Museum. The artist's ashes rest there in an ancient Mexican urn. Kahlo's work hangs not only in the Louvre but in many other museums in Europe, the United States, Asia, and, of course, Mexico. Two films, starring Ofelia Medina in Mexico and Salma Hayek in the U.S., played to millions. The Legacy Walk in Chicago, an outdoor display celebrating LGBTQ history, features her name. Her portrait appears on the front of the Mexican 500-peso note, Rivera's on the back side.

Despite all her troubles, the petite, raven-haired artist with the dark, flashing eyes gave the world pictures powerfully connecting the realms of reality and magic. Kahlo led intertwined lives of intense pain and equally intense art. A few days before her death, she wrote a final entry in her diary: "I hope the exit is joyful… and I hope never to come back…Frida."

The Blue House, Kahlo's childhood home.

Pinin Brambilla Barcilon in front of Leonardo da Vinci's *Last Supper*.

10. INCH BY INCH....

Pinin Brambilla Barcilon, Conservator, Italy (1925-   )

Pressure? How about cleaning the most famous art work in the world, centuries old, painted on a damp, crumbling wall, while the paint is flaking off and any mistake can knock off another bit? While the whole world watches on video?

Fifty-three year-old Pinin Brambilla Barcilon leans forward, peering through a large magnifying lens at a paint chip no bigger than her thumbnail. Six feet off the floor on a scaffold of pipes and planks, she works under the heat and glare of multiple spotlights illuminating the room like a film set. Laying a bit of special Japanese paper on the flake, she brushes on some cleaning solvent, then waits as the solvent softens any grime or old varnish on the paint flake. When Barcilon carefully peels off the tissue, the original bright blue of the flake is revealed —for the first time since it was originally painted in 1498.

A petite woman with keen dark eyes and a strong jaw, Barcilon has short, strawberry blonde hair. Like an expert surgeon, she makes only gentle, deft movements with her hands, careful not to destroy what she's trying to save.

A group of tourists enters, whispering, shooting photos, asking questions of their guide. Their chatter echoes in the room. Because the work is so famous, the *Last Supper* is always on display. TV crews and news reporters from all over the world are following how Barcilon is doing. After all, she's working on Leonardo Da Vinci's *Last Supper*, his most famous work after the *Mona Lisa*. But it's in deep trouble, peeling off the wall. If something isn't done, it will be lost forever. "It's a rescue operation," says Barcilon.

But can she save it? Can anyone, in fact? Or is the hourly, daily, weekly, monthly close work simply too late?

The *Last Supper* is a *fresco* (wall painting) that since 1498 has decorated one entire wall of the refectory, or dining room, of a red brick monastery in the city of Milan, Italy. The refectory is no larger than the seating area in an average Starbuck's. Just outside, traffic zooms down the busy Corso Magenta. With its neat gardens and green cloister, the monastery is an island of peace in the capital of fashion.

*   *   *

Born in Milan in 1925, Barcilon set out to be an architect, but along the way took a job with the famous Italian architect and designer Gio Ponti. She painted

flowers on the tablecloths he created. When she assisted a professional conservator, Mauro Pellicioli, she
fell in love with the practice of restoration. Pellicioli worked on Leonardo's *Last Supper* from 1951-1953,
using sticky shellac to reattach
many flakes and a knife to scrape
off layers of earlier repainting.

As a young woman Barcilon
worked with Pellicioli on restorations all over Italy, on important art

A young Barcilon works on a mural.

by the most famous painters, including Piero della Francesca, Caravaggio, and
Titian. She helped restore the frescoes of Giotto in the Arena Chapel in Padua,
which cover every wall and the ceiling with scenes from the lives of Christ and
the Virgin Mary. Here Barcilon gained valuable experience in working with
very old paintings in equally old buildings. Today, as one art writer says, "Barcilon is one of the world's foremost authorities on the conservation of Renaissance frescoes."

Although the *Last Supper* is an art work, Barcilon's restoration began scien-
tifically. Old paintings and frescoes, like some birthday cakes, may have many

Leonardo da Vinci's large but very damaged *Last Supper*.

layers. Most aren't visible to the naked eye. To study these, Barcilon first removed several small chips of paint. She set these in chunks of resin to protect them. Then Barcilon used a special, magnifying stratigraphic camera to photograph them. Studying the photos under a microscope, where they might be magnified two hundred twenty times, she could see them clearly. The first, lowest layer of Leonardo's fresco was a mix of lime and sand, brushed onto the bare wall to make a smooth first surface. Next came a layer of white lead.

Leonardo painted his colors on the third layer. Light falling on the painting "bounces" off the white layers back up through the colors above them, making the whole scene bright. It's as if light shone from behind the painting.

But paintings or frescoes may have even more layers than those laid down by their artists. Previous restorers may have painted over the original colors because they faded. They may have brushed on transparent glue or applied varnish to protect the colors. Then there may be mold from dampness, candle smoke from the days before electricity, grease from a nearby kitchen, plain old dirt and grime from air pollution, house dust, and finally even cobwebs. Seen under a microscope, these bands add more layers to the "cake." Under special kinds of light, Barcilon could identify what they were made of. Under ultraviolet light, for instance, varnish fluoresces. That is, it flames up as bright blue or green. "Raking light," where a strong beam of ordinary light sweeps the picture from the side, causes bumps and hollows in the surface to throw shadows. The painting may appear smooth to the naked eye, but when magnified its surface may look as rough as the moon. Barcilon could see where she had to be particularly careful. Finally, Barcilon's assistants drilled out tiny core samples in order to examine the layers physically. They even poked miniature TV cameras into hairline cracks in the wall to see how solid it still was.

After this extensive technical analysis, Barcilon made some important decisions.

Because the *Last Supper* is a fresco, painted on a wall, it could not be moved to a safer location to be worked on. But the wall was old and damp, and the air in Milan was thick with smog from cars and trucks. So Barcilon oversaw the installation of air conditioning and dehumidifying fans to stabilize the temperature, humidity, and atmospheric pressure in the room. Now visitors had to pass through a series of rooms, like air locks on a space ship, to see the painting.

Next, Barcilon ordered a drastic reduction in the number and length of visits. Today, no more than twenty-five people are allowed into the refectory at any one time. Visits are limited to fifteen minutes, so the dampness of the visitors' breath and their perspiration, no matter how limited, cannot dramatically affect the humidity in the room.

Then Barcilon had to decide exactly what she would do. Her job would be twofold: first cleaning, then restoring. But Barcilon had to ask herself some important questions. If the colors in an area have faded or darkened with grime, should she clean them, or would it be better—safer—to just leave them alone? Exactly what cleaning materials would she use? What solvents, papers, swabs? Was she sure they would help, not harm, what was there? Restoring, Barcilon's second task, could include repainting to brighten faded colors or filling blank spaces where the paint had flaked off completely. But how much paint could she add before the *Last Supper* stopped being Leonardo's and became hers? If a patch had no paint at all, should she add what she thought was the right color or just leave the area bare? Whether cleaning or repainting, a tremor of her hand could cause more paint to flake off: how could she be sure to improve, not ruin, this priceless art work?

Once Barcilon answered these questions for herself, she donned her smock, gathered her materials, and mounted the scaffold that brought her close to the work. She swung into place the circular magnifying glass on the moveable arm beside her. Close up, she later reflected, "the entire, uneven surface was composed of endless small islands of color."

Twenty-nine feet wide by fifteen feet high, almost twelve feet off the floor at its highest point, the scene depicts a life and death moment. The fresco shows Christ and the twelve Apostles seated at a long table in Jerusalem the night before his crucifixion. It's the very instant when

Barcilon and assistants on scaffolding needed to reach the higher points on the fresco.

he announces shocking news: "One of you will betray me." One of them will turn him in to the Roman authorities, who will take him away to be killed.

It wasn't unusual for convents and monasteries to have a *Last Supper* in their dining halls. Nuns and monks often ate in silence, so they could contemplate the Biblical figures who were also dining. But Leonardo's scene has special features. You can see what's on the table—fish, oranges, bread, even an eel (unnoticed until Barcilon's restoration). Most *Last Suppers* are solemn and static, but Leonardo's is not. The Apostles rise up in surprise. Heads rear back. Hands gesture. Glances fly in all direction. Leonardo makes all the Apostles look different. They're thirteen individuals, with dramatic gestures and expressions all their own. Only one person, Judas, the traitor, sits still. Leonardo shows him tightly grasping the bag with the thirty pieces of silver that are his payoff.

The work was probably commissioned by Lodovico Sforza, the duke of Milan, who also signed up for a statue of his father Francesco on horseback. A clay model of the horse, twenty-four feet high, intended to be the largest equestrian statue in the world, was as far as Leonardo got. He was busy on the *Last Supper* at the same time.

Leonardo was well known for working slowly. The *Last Supper* took him four years. Born on April 15, 1452 near the village of Vinci in what is now Tuscany, Leonardo was a true genius, however: not only an accomplished artist, but also a brilliant military tactician, inventor, scientist, and engineer. His notebooks included drawings for a 33-barreled "machine gun," a robotic knight, a mechanical lion, a parachute, a diving suit, a submarine, and a helicopter, in addition to an "ornithopter" that flew by beating its wings.

But Leonardo made two big mistakes with the *Last Supper*. While he'd made many paintings on canvas, he'd never actually tried a fresco before. The proper, time-honored way was to start with a wall of fresh, wet plaster, composed of limestone "slaked," or soaked, in water to a texture halfway between cream cheese and mayonnaise. Then you painted on this surface. When the water in the mix evaporated, the plaster turned back into stone, "freezing" the paint within it forever. Frescoes made this way last for hundreds of years with few problems and little fading. Leonardo's first mistake was to use dry wall, so his paints did not bond with the wall, they just sat on it. His second mistake was not to use the traditional fresco paint mix of pigment and lime water. Instead, Leonardo used tempera mixed with oil paint. Oil was a new medium from the North, the latest thing. Because it didn't dry quickly, an artist could take more time with his brush. But tempera, pigment mixed with "sticky" egg yolk, was for painting on wood panels or canvas, not for frescoes. Leonardo's mix didn't stick well to the dry wall on which it was just sitting. Leonardo was a brilliant innovator in many areas, but here his attempts to be original undermined his own efforts.

People think the *Last Supper* fresco captures a key Bible scene better than any other version on earth. However, because Leonardo painted the scene over five hundred years ago on a dry wall with experimental paint, the colors have been flaking off the wall almost from the day Leonardo finished it. By the time Barcilon got to it, huge areas had no paint at all.

Damage threatened the *Last Supper* almost right away—and kept threatening:

1517: Because the paint was already peeling off, Leonardo returned to attempt to repaint the scene completely. It's unclear how much he actually accomplished.

1652: Monks cut a door through the fresco, destroying Jesus' feet.

1726-1954: Workers on seven different "restorations" overpainted peeled or faded areas with colors that didn't match the originals.

1796: Napoleon's invasion of Italy brought French soldiers to Milan. Some were billeted at the monastery. Anti-Catholic revolutionaries, they threw rocks, bricks, and horse manure at the painting. Mounting ladders, they scratched out the Apostles' eyes.

1800: The refectory was flooded with two feet of water that soaked into, then up, the wall, producing a skim of green mold that loosened more of the paint.

1943: On the night of August 15 in World War II, Americans and British warplanes bombed Milan. Although they did not make a direct hit on the *Last Supper* itself, they destroyed much of the monastery. The entire outside wall of the refectory collapsed, exposing the *Last Supper* to rain, snow, sleet, and summer heat for the two years it took to rebuild the room.

1951-1953: Barcilon's mentor Mauro Pellicioli restored the painting as best as he could, given the technology of his time.

After all this, now it was Barcilon's turn. The year was 1978, exactly 480 years after Leonardo first laid his colors down.

First, Barcilon embarked on the lengthy process of cleaning. This was the truly grueling, exacting work. On a good day Barcilon cleaned an area the size of a postage stamp. As she said at the time, "I often have to clean the same piece a second time, or even a third or a fourth. The top section of the painting is impregnated with glue. The middle is filled with wax. There are six different kinds of plaster and several varnishes, lacquers and gums. What worked on the top section doesn't work in the middle. And what worked in the middle won't work on the bottom. It's enough to make a person want to shoot herself."

Detail of the head of Jesus, showing cracking, peeling, dirt, and the crumbling wall beneath.

Of course she was kidding. Barcilon was really a calm, steady, persevering worker who just kept working away until the truly original colors could be seen and the facial expressions of the figures were revealed in detail. And cleaning was of course just her first task.

Barcilon also tried to repaint faded flakes and bare areas. Using water and lime paints that she had matched as carefully as she could to the original colors on the wall, she covered one empty patch after another, dab after painstaking dab. When you look at the painting, you see areas of her colors besides areas of Leonardo's original paint. Her colors are less bright than his, but together the two create an overall image more complete than before.

Barcilon always said she enjoyed her work, calling her task "a privilege.... Each day," she said, "proved a new and engrossing experience...." Nonetheless she developed back problems from the constant stooping. Her eyesight suffered. And as one reporter observed, "In addition to the technical aspects, Mrs. Barcilon's story is especially telling for the personal details of her life and how she had to struggle with a society that put a lot of pressure on a working mother, and a husband who complained about not having his wife at home on weekends, along with the financial and bureaucratic barriers of the project and the huge burden of responsibility that it represented." There were daily distractions, too. Barcilon recalled, "I remember the great noise of visiting tourists, which kept me from concentrating."

On top of all this there were the critics, watching her every move via TV feed. All over Italy and the world as well, opinion was sharply divided. Attempt to do what Barcilon was doing or just leave the painting alone? Some critics took to the media to try to stop her. Michael Daly of ArtWatch UK said the restoration was completely unnecessary "even in terms of conservation." Professor James Beck of Columbia University said of Barcilon and her team, "they scraped everything away and repainted it themselves." The fresco, according to Beck, is now "18-20 percent Leonardo and 80 percent by the restorer. She repainted the head of Christ, which I thought was pretty drastic. People seem to like it, but that's not the issue. It's a post-modern painting now and not a Renaissance painting." A newspaper columnist wrote, "The *Last Supper* is now a first-rate example of Barcilon's work. It is not a Leonardo."

Exterior of the monastery of Santa Maria delle Grazie, home of the *Last Supper*.

Barcilon never complained. As she explained later, "You know that when you are in the front line you will be hit first. But I had taken on that commitment and went ahead, trying not to listen to the malicious criticism so as not to lose focus." Barcilon said further, and more deeply, "The relationship that is established with the work that is restored is a relationship of empathy, not only and simply an emotional participation, but a capacity (which is exercised with the mind and the heart) to identify with the work of art, to perceive its intimate structure, to capture its soul, the most authentic truth."

Probably only someone as strong as Barcilon could have withstood the constant public criticism and still be willing to try to save the *Last Supper*. For twenty-one years her working world was reduced to a single wall in an old dining hall in a small brick monastery on an unexceptional side street in a noisy city. She completed the restoration on May 28, 1999, 7,665 days after she started. Thanks to her ability to bring rigorous, up-to-date science and her own remarkable patience to a work of art that had literally almost evaporated into thin air, the *Last Supper* survives. Over four hundred thousand people visit each year. For the price of a movie ticket, anyone can see it.

Or what remains of it. Pinin Brambilla Barcilon herself, now ninety-four, admits, "While the restoration has produced positive results, it has also forced us to confront the painful truth that much of Leonardo's original work is irrevocably lost." But not for lack of effort on her part. Barcilon devoted her life to saving it.

11. HOW MANY LIVES CAN YOU LEAD?

Faith Ringgold, Painter, Quilter, Writer, Activist, USA, (1930-   )

Traveling underground in total darkness, the subway train jerks its riders back and forth, side to side as it hurtles through the tunnels under New York City. It lurches into every turn, wheels screeching like a knife on steel, until suddenly it slows and brakes and stops at the 125th Street station in Harlem, and its riders get off. As they work their way

Faith Ringgold.

Harlem's world-famous
Apollo Theater.

through the crowd on the platform, they are met by bursts of bright color on the white tiles covering the walls. These are Faith Ringgold's mosaic murals of African-American heroes and heroines "flying home" to their Harlem neighborhood.

Above a mosaic depiction of the Apollo Theater, where everyone from Michael Jackson to the Supremes, Stevie Wonder, and Elton John has performed, fly singing greats Dinah Washington ("Unforgettable") and Billie Holiday ("I've Got My Love to Keep Me Warm"). Opera singer Marian Anderson, wearing a long red dress and matching heels, glides over the Harlem Opera House accompanied by fellow singer (and actor) Paul Robeson. Track and field star Jesse Owens leaps up from the Berlin stadium where he triumphed in the 1936 Olympics, four gold medals around his neck. Author Zora Neale Hurston (*Their Eyes Were Watching God*) flies above the Schomburg Library in a wide-brimmed straw hat, arms outstretched, a big smile on her face. Civil rights leaders Dr. Martin Luther King, Jr. and Malcolm X soar above Harlem's elite Theresa Hotel.

Delightfully surprising, these airborne singers, artists, musicians, ministers, politicians, and athletes are typical of Ringgold's lively, whimsical style. This art is not in a museum but out where people can see and enjoy it every day on their way to school or work. And the figures come with a clear message: remarkable people call Harlem home.

One such person is Faith Ringgold herself. But if she appeared in her own mural, she would be hard to categorize. Of course she's a muralist, but she's also a painter, quilter, writer, illustrator, educator, activist, mother, and wife. She is successful in all of these roles. How on earth did she grow so many lives?

*   *   *

Born in Harlem on October 8, 1930 to Willi Posey and Andrew Jones, Faith Willi Jones suffered asthma attacks as a child. She spent her first and second grade years at home. Her mother gave her crayons, paper, and bits of fabric to play with, and Faith's creative spirit flourished. Eventually she was able to return to formal education, graduating from Morris High School in 1948 at eighteen. But when she arrived at the School of Liberal Arts of the City College of New York intending to major in art, officials told her that as a woman she could not. In order to study art, Faith had to enroll in the School of Education. She could major in art only if she also minored in education. The message was clear: it was okay for a woman to be a teacher, but not okay to declare herself an artist.

On November 1, 1950, in the fall of her junior year, Faith married classical and jazz pianist Robert Earl Wallace. Her two daughters were both born in 1952, Michele on January 4 and Barbara on December 15. In 1954 Ringgold, now twenty-four, divorced Wallace, who had developed an addiction to heroin. Ringgold graduated from City College with a B.S. in Fine Art and Education in 1955. She took a teaching job at the Harriet Beecher Stowe School in Harlem.

In her apartment Ringgold created a small studio for herself, where she painted. She squeezed out her painting time between her responsibilities as a teacher and mother. When she returned to City College to study for a graduate degree in art, it became clear that she had a special ability to pursue several paths at once. This talent reappeared in the many different media she mastered as a mature artist.

In 1959, after receiving her master's degree, Ringgold traveled to Europe with her mother and two young daughters. The young painter was thrilled to see and study world-famous paintings and sculptures in the art museums of France and Italy. However, the trip was interrupted by news of her older brother Andrew's death. A member of a Harlem gang, he had died of a heroin overdose. Ringgold and her family returned to the U. S. for his funeral.

On May 19, 1962, the artist, now thirty-two, remarried, to Burdette "Birdie" Ringgold, an automobile executive. She continued to teach in the New York City school system, now at Walton High School in the Bronx. At this time Ringgold was painting still lifes and landscapes. One day she and Birdie took some of her paintings to show Manhattan gallery owner Ruth White, hoping White would decide to exhibit her work. But White turned her down. She told Ringgold, "You can't do this." What did White mean? On the way home, the artist discussed the question with her husband: "I said to him, 'You know something? I think what she's saying is—it's the 1960s, all hell is breaking loose all over, and you're painting flowers and leaves. You can't do that. Your job is to tell your story. Your story has to come out of your life, your environment, who you are, where you come from.'" Ringgold was living in the Sixties, the time of the greatest struggle for civil rights in U. S. history. White thought that story should be her subject, not flowers and fruit and rolling hills.

The summer of 1967 became known as "the long hot summer" because of race riots, which included the burning and looting of stores in numerous American cities. Black anger at racial injustice, abusive policing, and lack of employment spilled into the streets. Detroit, Atlanta, Boston, Buffalo, Birmingham, Tampa, Rochester, and many other cities suffered. In her autobiography, *We Flew Over the Bridge*, Ringgold noted, "The climate of America was changing in the summer of 1967. We were moving out of the civil rights period and were at the start of the Black Revolution." Ringgold's art was changing, too. No more still lifes, no more landscapes. People. Upset, energized, hurting people, reflecting the racial tensions of the time.

On December 19, 1967, a show of this new work opened at the prestigious Spectrum Gallery on 57th Street in midtown Manhattan. Ringgold's eight foot by six foot painting, *The Flag is Bleeding*, got a lot of attention. Three people—a white man, a white woman, and a black man with a knife—stand arm in arm behind a bloody American flag that fills the canvas. Blood streams from the black man's heart. Part of the message? We're all in this together. And we're in pain. Ringgold

Ringgold's *The Flag is Bleeding*,
a breakthrough work for American art.

was thirty-seven years old when she painted the work. She said, "It would be impossible for me to picture the American flag as just a flag, as if that is the whole story. I need to communicate my relationship with this flag based on my experience as a black woman in America."

Four years later Ringgold produced a two-panel mural for the cafeteria of the women's prison at Riker's Island, just outside New York City. Called *For The Women's House*, it showed a female doctor, minister, dancer, musician, construction worker, police officer, and U.S. President. Ringgold hoped to inspire and uplift the women incarcerated there, showing them images of what they might aspire to be.

The Seventies were also a time when Ringgold took part in protests against New York museums for not including women and artists of color in their collections and exhibitions. With others she demanded that the Museum of Modern Art on 53rd Street build an addition in honor of Martin Luther King, Jr. that would be devoted to works by artists of color. Her group presented a list of twenty questions, among them: "Does the museum's collection of over 30,000 works of art include the works of black and Puerto Rican artists? If so, which, and how many?" Ringgold and her friends knew the answer, of course: few, if any. But they wanted others to know as well. African-Americans and Puerto Ricans were sizeable segments of New York City's population.

While the wing wasn't built, the museum did add two African-Americans to its Board of Trustees and mounted exhibitions by two black artists. Ringgold also participated in demonstrations at the Whitney Museum of American Art in New York demanding that women artists be represented equally with men. As a result, twenty women and two black sculptors, Betye Saar and Barbara Chase-Riboud, were included in an exhibition of sculpture that year, the first black women ever to exhibit at the Whitney. Ringgold also co-founded a women's art group, "Where We At." Among its activities were art classes for inmates at area prisons. Should artists get involved in politics? Or should they stand aside, simply making beautiful works? To Ringgold, the answer was clear.

In the summer of 1972 Ringgold visited the Rijksmuseum in Amsterdam, Holland. Now forty-two, she was struck by a display of Nepali *thangkas*. These colorful Buddhist works were painted on silk, not canvas stretched on wooden

A *thangka* from Bhutan.

frames, like her paintings. Now Ringgold's art evolved again, as she moved into soft materials and fabrics.

Touring West Africa in 1976 and 1977, Ringgold continued her exploration of textile art. The colorful Kente cloths and Dahomey appliqués spoke to her. Mixing what she had seen in Amsterdam and Africa together with her own heritage, she came to quilts. Decorated with scenes and figures, "story quilts" were originally created communally by groups of African-American women. Ringgold explains: "I went to West Africa in the 1970's and returned home inspired to write my memoir, *We Flew Over the Bridge: The Memoirs of Faith Ringgold*.... During that time I wrote and painted story quilts... working in collaboration with my mother, a dressmaker and fashion designer. We made our first quilt in 1980." Willi Posey had trained at the Fashion Institute of Technology in New York. Ringgold was fifty when they finished *Echoes of Harlem*. The women used finely woven duck canvas as the base, painting it with acrylics, then adding squares of upholstery fabric for further decoration.

As Ringgold's daughter Michele explains, "Quilting she had learned from her mother (Mme. Willi Posey), who had learned it from her mother (Ida Matilda Posey) and her grandmother (Betsy Bingham) in Palatka and Jacksonville, Florida, who had learned it from their female forebears who had been weavers, quilters and seamstresses for their families and their communities."

In 1981 Ringgold's mother died of a heart attack, but the artist continued making story quilts. Her 1983 quilt *Who's Afraid of Aunt Jemima?* confronted the African-American figure used by the Quaker Oats company to sell maple syrup and pancakes.

Aunt Jemima was a racist stereotype from 19th century minstrel shows, wearing a kerchief and an apron. Ringgold's brightly colored quilt had thirteen images showing a new "Jemima" as the successful owner of a restaurant in Harlem, the head of her own business. The artist made it clear that black women now had opportunities to create their own professional lives. In addition to images, nine squares of written material told the story of the new Jemima's new life.

Ringgold's 1988 quilt *Tar Beach* became the seed of her first children's book. Nearly six feet by six feet, the quilt shows a family enjoying supper on a Manhattan rooftop. Under a deep blue, star-studded sky, the George Washington Bridge is visible in the background. Two children lie on a towel on the asphalt surface, the "tar beach" of their imagination. One of them is eight year-old Cassie Louise Lightfoot. Cassie is also shown flying over the bridge in her imagination. As Cassie herself explains in words painted on the quilt, "Only eight years old and in the third grade and I can fly. That means I am free to go wherever I want to for the rest of my life."

Ringgold says about Cassie, "The stars lift her up, and she flies over the city. She claims the buildings as her own—even the union building, so her father won't have to worry anymore about not being allowed to join just because his father was not a member. As Cassie learns, anyone can fly. 'All you need is somewhere to go you can't get to any other way. The next thing you know, you're flying above the stars.'" In real life, too, Ringgold clearly meant. She says, "My women are actually flying; they are just free, totally." In a YouTube video, Ringgold shows how she made the quilt, which is now in the Guggenheim Museum on Fifth Avenue.

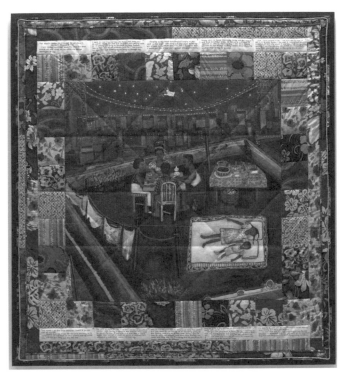

Tar Beach quilt, showing Cassie soaring over the George Washington Bridge.

Ringgold's book *Tar Beach*, based on this quilt, appeared in 1991, when the artist was sixty-one. The book won the Ezra Jack Keats New Writer Award and the Coretta Scott King Award for Illustration. It was a runner-up for the

Caldecott Medal, the most prestigious illustrator's award in the country. Ringgold eventually wrote and illustrated seventeen children's books.

In 1992 Ringgold and Birdie moved out of Harlem to the suburb of Englewood, New Jersey, just across the George Washington Bridge. But Ringgold did not stop being an educator. Although she retired from the New York City schools in 1973, she later taught at Wilson College in Chambersburg, Pennsylvania and at the University of California in San Diego from 1984-2002, until she retired at seventy-two.

At eighty-nine Ringgold is still active. Few American artists work in so many media. She has created murals, books, illustrations, quilts, poems, paintings, songs, posters, dolls, even a set of playing cards. Nor do many artists reach such diverse audiences. Hundreds of thousands of people see Ringgold's work every year. Even if they don't go to museums, they take the subway to Harlem,

Tar Beach 2 quilt, in the Philadelphia Museum of Art, continues the story of Cassie.

buy her books for their children, and read her memoir.

Ringgold's work is in the most selective museums, including, in the U.S. alone, the Guggenheim Museum, Metropolitan Museum of Art, Museum of Modern Art, Museum of Fine Arts Boston, Baltimore Museum, and the St. Louis Art Museum. She has received twenty-three honorary degrees, including a Doctor of Fine Arts degree from City College, which initially barred her from majoring in art.

In 2007 the artist received perhaps her highest honor when the State of California named a new K-8 school in Hayward after her: the Faith Ringgold School of Arts and Science. What a wonderful place for this multi-talented artist to "fly home" to, in her imagination. Just like the soaring figures in her very own subway mural....

12. DARING PHOTOGRAPHER

Annie Leibovitz, Photographer, USA (1949-   )

Risking her life with every step, Annie Leibovitz walked out onto the massive chrome eagle's head jutting out from the sixty-first story of New York's Chrysler Building like a gargoyle from a cathedral. It was barely two feet wide and only eight feet long. The chrome was polished, smooth, slick. Leibovitz, age forty-two, wore no safety harness or wire, just her usual black shirt and slacks and rubber-soled clogs. She had her camera. An assistant, Robert Bean, stood by to hand her extra film. From below, on the sidewalk, the sounds of taxi horns and buses were audible. A light wind sighed past. The view was spectacular, across the entire city and the Hudson River to New Jersey. But a strong gust of wind, a missed step, a wobble, and Leibovitz would have fallen to her death....

Chrysler Building eagles, out onto one of which Leibovitz fearlessly walked, 700 feet above the sidewalk below.

On another eagle's head, at an opposite corner, dancer David Parsons appeared. Athletic, strong, with a head of thick dark hair and handsome features, Parsons was known for his daring stage leaps. Artsy *Vanity Fair* magazine put it, "Heights held no terror for him." But Parsons later admitted that *this* height, some seven hundred feet above the sidewalk, not just six feet above a stage floor, was different. About halfway through the shooting he suffered a moment of panic. "The danger of having an anxiety attack is that you get dizzy," he said, "and I really needed to just get control again." It took him twenty-five minutes to recover.

Leibovitz wore her blond hair shoulder length, as usual. She is tall, with a broad, open face, a wide, mobile mouth that can take a variety of shapes—more often than not a hearty grin—and blue-gray eyes that don't miss a thing. She is always scanning her surroundings, looking for that next shot.

That afternoon on the Chrysler Building, biographer Vicki Goldberg explains: "The only time she lets someone hold her is when she puts one foot way out on the gargoyle's head, and once she feels secure there she makes her assistant let go and stands free above the New York skyline with the wind whipping at her trousers."

When Leibovitz was ready on her eagle, she called across the way to Parsons, who crawled out and lay flat on his stomach, stretched full length on his own eagle's head, gazing pensively out over the great city, naked. The setting sun on his muscular body lit him with a warm glow. And Leibovitz shot. The photograph was featured in *Vanity Fair*. And Leibovitz, Parsons, and Bean went home alive that evening.

The courage, the boldness, that drove her to take that risk in order to make a photograph of Parsons, underlies an astonishing career. Leibovitz has recorded some of the most amazing talents, bands, actors, and celebrities in the world, from Whoopi Goldberg and the Rolling Stones to Meryl Streep and Jennifer Lawrence. She has photographed Queen Elizabeth of England and Presidents George W. Bush and Barack Obama.

Leibovitz's path to excellence and fame was hardly planned or predictable. But it was always bold.

* * *

Born Anna-Lou Leibovitz on October 2, 1949 in suburban Waterbury, Connecticut, she had five brothers and sisters. Because Annie's father was a lieutenant colonel in the Air Force, the family often moved. Once they drove all the way from Fairbanks, Alaska to Ft. Hood, Texas in their station wagon, not even stopping at motels.

Leibovitz made her first serious commitment to the arts in 1970, when she was twenty-one, enrolling at the San Francisco Art Institute to study painting. She had just returned from working in a kibbutz in Israel. In San Francisco, Leibovitz recalls, "I took a photography workshop, and that's when I decided that this was what I wanted to do. Photography suited me. I was a young and unformed person and impatient. Photography seemed like a faster medium than painting."

But a huge question was, could she even make a living as a photographer? And if so, what would that look like?

Luckily, Leibovitz got a job as a photographer that same year, with a little start-up magazine in San Francisco calling itself *Rolling Stone*. It covered rock and roll, a young, unconventional form of music. The magazine's publishers thought it might have a future. Now a famous pop culture publication with a worldwide audience, *Rolling Stone* first dealt just with singers, bands, and their milieu. Leibovitz said of her job, "It sounds exciting but no one at school thought it was a good thing. Photography was taught as an art. You weren't supposed to sell anything. The other students looked at me with disdain. I felt alone—very alone." Her first cover photo, June 11, 1970, was of an anti-Vietnam War rally. "Seeing that image on the newsstands is a moment that will stay with me forever."

Leibovitz worked for *Rolling Stone* for the next thirteen years. In 1975 she actually toured with the Rolling Stones *band* (no connection with the magazine). She noted, "A rock and roll tour is unnatural. You're moving through time and space too fast. The experience is extreme. There is the bigness of the performance and then the isolation and loneliness that follows." As Leibovitz's photos appeared on the covers, she became famous. It didn't hurt that most of her photographs were of celebrities, whether from the music world or from film, dance, the arts in general, even beyond.

Leibovitz's portraits are particularly memorable because she tries hard to be original. How can she show a well-known figure in a fresh way? Attention-getting but sincere, revealing but not intrusive? Often Leibovitz places her subject in an unusual or elaborate setting. She says, "As soon as you engage someone their face changes. They become animated. They forget about being photographed. Their minds become occupied and they look more interesting." Leibovitz always tries to get to the "real person" behind the public persona.

Five special photographs mark Leibovitz's progress. Perhaps the most famous is that of John Lennon and Yoko Ono, which appeared on *Rolling Stone's* cover in January, 1981. Leibovitz was thirty-two. She took it on December 8, 1980 in the couple's apartment in the Dakota apartment building overlooking Central Park in New York City. The photograph was a shocker because Annie posed the two hugging, with Lennon naked. It's not very revealing: he's shown from the side. *Rolling Stone* had wanted just him for

Annie Leibovitz with Gloria Steinem in front of Leibovitz's exhibition, "Women: New Portraits," in London.

the cover, but when Leibovitz arrived, Lennon insisted that Ono, a conceptual artist, be included. Just five hours later, Mark David Chapman shot and killed Lennon outside in the park.

Leibovitz reflects, "I was stunned by the fact that he was killed that evening; I didn't want to sell the picture.... Suddenly, that photograph has a story. You're looking at it and thinking it's their last kiss, or they're saying goodbye. You can make up all sorts of things about it. I think it's amazing when there's a lot of levels to a photograph."

That same year Leibovitz also photographed Meryl Streep. Streep's film *The French Lieutenant's Woman* had just been released. Leibovitz recalls, "Meryl was uncomfortable with all the attention she was getting.... She came in [to my studio] and talked about how she didn't want to be anybody; she was nobody, just an actress. There were a lot of clown books lying around the studio and some white makeup left over.... I told Meryl that she didn't have to be anybody in particular, and I suggested that maybe she would like to put on whiteface. To be a mime. That set her at ease. She had a role to play. It was her idea to pull at her face."

The published result, another *Rolling Stone* cover, is a close-up of Streep's face with chalk-white skin and rose-pink lips. She's tugging at her right cheek and left eyebrow, making her face look rubbery. Streep wears a blank expression. Because she is known to be such an expressive actress, the whole picture is a surprise, just the kind of effect Leibovitz seeks. She later said, "I think she felt really good that she could hide underneath [the makeup]."

Three years later, in 1984, Leibovitz moved to *Vanity Fair* magazine. She was now thirty-five and living in the Greenwich Village section of New York City. For a *Vanity Fair* cover shot of Whoopi Goldberg, who was just becoming known, she posed the actor in a bathtub full of white milk. Leibovitz and her assistants heated gallons of the liquid to fill it. Goldberg sinks below the surface, until you can see only her head, arms, and legs. Leibovitz recalls, "I kind of thought that she would be sitting up in the bath and scrubbing herself. She sat back and suddenly we had a very strong image. It was a total surprise." When Goldberg stuck out her tongue and laughed, Leibovitz took the picture. "Things happen in front of you," says Leibovitz. "That's perhaps the most wonderful and mysterious aspect of photography... what does happen a lot is that as soon as you say it's over, the subject will feel relieved and suddenly look great. And then you keep shooting...." The simple contrast of dark skin and white milk is striking, particularly in a *color* photograph. Even more so is the whole idea: a grown, famous woman on her back in a bathtub with arms and legs waving. Almost as funny as the real Goldberg herself.

Leibovitz began seeing the renowned thinker and writer Susan Sontag in 1989. The photographer had just turned forty. Sontag was influential as an essayist. Her book *Against Interpretation* challenged readers to think about how they looked at modern art. *Illness as Metaphor* argued for deeper sympathy for cancer patients. Over the succeeding years the relationship between Leibovitz and Sontag deepened, although they never lived together. Instead, they kept separate apartments near each other, supporting each emotionally and professionally. Leibovitz took many photographs of Susan at her home and on their trips together.

For a 1991 *Vanity Fair* cover Leibovitz took what turned out to be a controversial image of Demi Moore. The actor had a movie coming out and was seven months pregnant. Leibovitz shot her in all sorts of outfits. She also made one nude photograph, initially meant just for Moore. In it the actor covers herself with her hands but shows her belly. Everyone, including Moore, loved it. The editors decided it should be the cover shot. When the issue

Controversial *Vanity Fair* magazine cover with Leibovitz's photo of actor Demi Moore.

was published, some newsstands wouldn't display the magazine. Many people considered it "scandalous" and "immoral."

"None of this was my intention," said Leibovitz, "although it's gratifying to think that the picture helped make pregnant women feel less awkward or embarrassed about their bodies." The reaction was less about the lack of clothes and more about the fact that a celebrity was presented without glamorous make-up, a skinny body, or fancy clothes. Instead Moore looked like an "ordinary" woman. Leibovitz was very conscious of not exploiting Moore in the shot: "Taking intimate pictures of family members and people to whom you are close is a privilege, and it bears a certain responsibility."

Leibovitz's courageous photography is not restricted to the world of culture. In 1993, at age forty-four, she traveled to Sarajevo, a city under siege in the Bosnian war, and in 1994, to Rwanda, a country that suffered an horrific civil war and genocide. In Sarajevo, Leibovitz shot her photographs, still emphasizing people, in hospitals, schools, and rubble-strewn streets. The opposite of her celebrity shots, they show people in terrible pain and suffering. Leibovitz says, "The city is at the bottom of a bowl created by a ring of mountains, and the Serbs [the enemy] sat in the mountains lobbing shells down. Snipers were picking people off at random… people from all walks of life. Death was random. The sound of gunfire and shelling went on all day." One of her photographs from Rwanda shows the bloody footprints of children on a church wall they tried to climb over to escape men from another ethnic group who came in to kill them with machetes.

Leibovitz's war photographs show the strength of the people as well as their pain. They are very different from her other work. The photographer was deeply moved by these experiences. "There's something intoxicating about being in a place where everything is stripped down to simple life and death," she says. "That's why journalists and photographers go from war to war. Everything else seems trivial."

In October of 2001, when she was fifty-two, Leibovitz gave birth to a daughter, Sarah Cameron, whom she and Sontag raised until Sontag's death from breast cancer in 2004. After the writer died, Leibovitz, who was usually very private about her, said to a journalist,

Essayist and intellectual Susan Sontag.

"Call us 'lovers'. I like 'lovers'... I loved Susan. I don't have a problem with that. I just had a problem with 'partner' or 'companion.' It just sounds like two little old ladies." This they were definitely not. Each in her way blazed new trails for women, as lesbians as well as artists.

Also in the family was a son, David, from Sontag's earlier marriage to writer Philip Rieff. And in 2005, when she was fifty-six, Leibovitz added twins Susan and Samuelle, born to a surrogate mother. Although it cannot have been easy to manage a household of four, sometimes five, along with a demanding career in celebrity photography, Leibovitz has been successful at both. Perhaps because she was bold and innovative as an artist, she could be equally courageous in her personal life. Without losing her sense of fun!

Leibovitz's *most* controversial photograph? The cover of the October 23, 2008 *Vanity Fair* showed a fifteen year-old Miley Cyrus, back turned, wearing just a white sheet. Many accused the magazine and Leibovitz, now fifty-nine, of exploiting a minor. Cyrus released a statement:" I took part in a photo shoot that was supposed to be 'artistic' and now, seeing the photographs and reading the story, I feel so embarrassed. I never intended for any of this to happen and I apologize to my fans who I care so deeply about." Leibovitz responded: "I'm sorry that my portrait of Miley has been misinterpreted. The photograph is a simple, classic portrait, shot with very little makeup, and I think it is very beautiful."

In December of 2011 the Obamas asked Leibovitz to shoot family photos. Their favorite showed the chief executive, Michelle, Malia, and Sasha at home in the White House just after a Sunday church service, arm in arm, affection-ate, smiling at the camera. Nothing sensational, just a clear, strong sense of their personalities.

The Obama Family at ease together in the White House.

Leibovitz met Meryl Streep again, in 2012, when *Vogue US* magazine asked the photographer to shoot her for its cover. Streep's film *Iron Lady*, about former British Prime Minister Margaret Thatcher, was about to be released. Streep agreed only if *Vogue* would also feature a distinguished group of women who were trying to establish a National Women's History Museum in Washington. She had signed on as their national spokesperson. The group included former Secretary of State Madeleine Albright, Maine Senator Susan Collins, and poet Maya Angelou. A deal was struck, so their group photo appears in the issue.

The cover photo shows Streep alone. Leibovitz posed her in a long grey dress on a seaside rock. Waves splash up beside Streep as her hair blows in the wind, and she laughs. It's a confident pose, a far cry from the hide-and-seek Streep of 1981. Perhaps it also reflects the progress of Leibovitz herself, the fearless gargoyle walker, from tag-along photographer at rock concerts to premier national chronicler. As it turned out, Annie Leibovitz never missed a step. And the seventy year-old photographer is still working today.

13. SEE WHAT I'M SAYING?

Jenny Holzer, Electronic Artist, USA (1950-   )

"EXPIRING FOR LOVE IS BEAUTIFUL BUT STUPID."

"YOUR OLDEST FEARS ARE THE WORST ONES."

Just two of Jenny Holzer's attention-getting statements.

Brilliant LED (light-emitting diode) lights—red, yellow, orange, blue—often scroll quickly past us on electronic message boards. We see them in sports stadiums and on highways. They generally say things related to where they're placed, such as "MAKE SOME NOISE!" or "NEW LAW: NO TEXTING WHILE DRIVING."

Holzer uses LED lights to make deeper points.

"EXPIRING FOR LOVE IS BEAUTIFUL BUT STUPID." For Romeo and Juliet? "YOUR OLDEST FEARS ARE THE WORST ONES." A challenge to grow?

"YOU CAN'T SEE OR TASTE MANY OF THE THINGS THAT KILL YOU NOW."

An environmental warning?

You really can't miss these messages when they flash by in letters four feet high, as Holzer's earliest display did, from a Spectacolor light board high above Times Square in New York City. That was in 1982, when she was thirty-two.

Holzer's message on abuse of power in Times Square.

A gaudy, noisy, crowded mishmash of Broadway, Seventh Avenue, and 42nd to 47th Streets, clogged with buses, trucks, taxis, cars, and bicycles, with drivers honking, tires squealing, and ticket sellers barking, Times Square is home to theaters, souvenir shops, cheap jewelry stores, fast food, tour hawkers, phone stores, and tourists from as far away as Beijing, Berlin, and Dubai. Add in teens from Hoboken, Harlem, and SoHo; street actors like Wonder Woman, Superman, Spider Man, the Statue of Liberty; and, most famous of all, on a traffic island in the middle of everything, the Naked Cowboy (who is not, really), with his Stetson, guitar, and Calvin Klein underwear. Above it all, mega LED message screens blaze ads for the latest films, plays, perfumes, lingerie, lotions, burgers, CDs, cars, and colas.

Holzer's 1982 messages alternated with an ad for Cheetos: "SEIZE THE CHEESE THAT GOES CRUNCH." Holzer posted, "IT IS MAN'S FATE TO OUT-SMART HIMSELF" and "TORTURE IS BARBARIC." No one else had thought of using electronics this way, as a giant post, or of displaying art in a busy commercial area instead of a hushed museum. Holzer made unfamiliar use of familiar technology. Today she still makes the common, uncommon.

Holzer's strong face is framed by long straight hair that falls well below her shoulders. She has large, dark eyes, a straight nose, and a wide mouth with thin lips that quickly breaks into a smile. She speaks in a quiet, thoughtful voice, pausing between thoughts. In public she generally dresses in black. She loves frozen organic pizzas.

She says of her scrolling messages, "I like it when the text is racing, and you don't know the source; I relied on this heavily with my own early work. I didn't want it attributed. I wanted people to think about what it meant as they read it, and not say, 'Oh, that's writing by a woman, or a such-and-such poem,' or even a poem—they just had to deal with the content."

* * *

Jenny Holzer was born in America's heartland, in Gallipolis, Ohio, on July 29, 1950. Her mother was a riding teacher who loved horses, her father a car salesman.

Jenny started out wanting to be a painter, entering Duke University in 1968, when she was eighteen. At Duke she imitated the work of abstract artists like Helen Frankenthaler and Mark Rothko. After transferring to the University of Chicago in 1970, where she practiced printmaking and drawing as well as painting, she moved again, to Ohio Christian University, from which she received her BFA in 1972. But she didn't feel she was done learning. Courses at the Rhode Island School of Design in 1975 led to an MFA a year later when she was twenty-six. Oddly, she had doubts about being an artist in the first place. "I tried to be a regular person. I thought I should be a lawyer. I was reassured by law. And still, to this day in the U.S., other than in pockets like New York City, it's not always considered a contribution to society to be an artist. Artists are characterized as odd and indulgent."

Moving to New York City, she surprised herself by leaving painting behind. She joined the artists' group Colab (short for Collaborative Projects), dedicated to creating group works for people who normally wouldn't see art, who might never go to a museum or gallery. Holzer explains, "A reason I first chose electronics is that people tend to look at them. I thought I should employ this fact to have people watch what they otherwise might not."

Clearly a signboard in Times Square or a bright LED message board meant instant exposure to thousands of people who didn't have to think about attending a "real" art show. And this led to the question of what Holzer should project. "I realized that people often could and would give the works a tiny bit of attention at best. I have had to think about the text selection and the media that were appropriate for holding people, getting to people just for a minute, in the street. One way was only to present short sentences, but then the challenge was to make sure the little short things were good and complex enough." That was the foundation for literally hundreds of presentations of her work around the world, including Sweden, France, Norway, Germany, Italy, Holland, and Spain, as well as the U.S.

In 1982 Holzer and her husband, the landscape painter Mike Glier, bought a farm in the village of Hoosick Falls, New York. They moved there in 1985, when she was thirty-five. Her daughter Lili was born three years later. Holzer says, "I had a child relatively late because I was pessimistic about the world and felt that I couldn't, in good conscience, have a baby. I was fearful of making a child hostage to fate in a more and more disturbing world... I hesitated until it was almost too late. But then I took the risk, and there she was." At the farm Holzer

Multiple projections
of messages reinforce
through repetition.
Inflammatory Wall.

keeps "retired" horses and ponies. Unlike her mother, she doesn't ride.

Holzer's many awards include honorary degrees from Williams College, RISD, Smith College, the New School, and Ohio University. In 1990, when she was forty, she became the first American woman to show in the Venice Biennale, one of the world's largest and most prestigious public exhibitions. There she won the coveted Leone d'Oro (gold lion) award. "My work might be like theater in that I hope there's an audience," she says. "I want color to suffuse the space and pulse and do all kinds of tricks."

Holzer also launches her messages onto the sides of big buildings at night using a projector with giant, incredibly bright lamps like the xenon machines in IMAX theaters. They're as bright as the spots that illuminate the rockets on the launch pads at the Kennedy Space Center. In 2004, when she was fifty-four, Holzer illuminated a protest poem this way by Polish writer and Nobel Prize winner Wislawa Szymborska. It shone on the outside of the Hotel Pennsylvania across the street from busy Penn Station and the sports venue Madison Square Garden. Holzer says, "People will read.... The crowd coming out of the Jay-Z concert and the Knicks game looked up and stayed with Szymborska, including the poem 'Torture.' About every 12th to 14th person looked; we sat and counted. That was interesting, because I always wonder if what I'm doing is useless, and just a nice and a pretty idea, or worse. But people will stop and read and talk."

That same year she also messaged a banner towed by a small airplane over New York City. In large black capital letters the sign read, "WHATEVER YOU ARE BE A GOOD ONE" and "ABUSE OF POWER COMES AS NO SURPRISE." This last statement is one of her most famous. Of course, it's a tweak of the famous comment by England's Lord Acton. Meant as a warning about giving leaders or governments too much authority, Acton cautioned, "Power tends to corrupt, and absolute power corrupts absolutely."

In 2005 on the exterior of the Bobst Library at New York University, Holzer projected pages of formerly top secret government documents declassified under the Freedom of Information Act. How much should we, the public, know? How much, for security reasons, should stay secret? These aren't easy questions to answer, Holzer suggests. For instance, we don't make our President's motorcade routes public, for security reasons. But because the Nazis kept the Holocaust secret, they perpetuated its horror. Holzer has a strong social conscience: "I think about bleak stuff, and the world keeps serving up war, terror, murder, totalitarianism, sex, kindness, and the most astounding beauty that needs reporting."

Holzer has created scrolling message boards in all sort of places, from famous art museums like the Guggenheim in New York, the Museum of Fine Arts in Boston, and the National Gallery of Canada in Ottawa, to more unlikely venues such as Amsterdam's Schiphol airport, the Isla de Esculturas in Ponteverda,

Spain, the Toray Building in Osaka, Japan, and the parking lot of the Aria Resort and Casino in Las Vegas.

Of course the point is to make passersby stop, look—and think. With a smile, Holzer says, "I write all my own clichés. I don't know whether that proves that I am really silly or stupid, but somehow it seemed that then I could address the particular issues that I wanted to. I could write them just on the topics that I thought were the big ones, and I thought if they were a little different from ones that you were familiar with, they might bring the point home better."

Color and brightness make Holzer's statements hard to ignore. *Installation for Bilbao.*

Holzer's art is different from any other artist's. It doesn't last. You can't take it home. She doesn't use paint, crayons, pastels, pencil, ink, watercolor, oil paint, clay, marble, bronze, wood, or steel. Instead, it's light. Technology. And her art is very, very public. It's not one object on one wall in one home or museum. And it has a definite social purpose: to "rival ignorance and violence with humor, kindness, and moral courage," she says on her website.

In the spring of 2017 she collaborated with Off-White menswear designer Virgil Abloh for a combined runway fashion show and projection at night on the facade of the famous stone Pitti Palace in Florence. She created huge projections of white capital letters spelling poems written by European refugees past and present, from Poland, Syria and other countries. One of the statements was from a World War II nurse: "ALTHOUGH YOUR BULLETS WILL TEAR APART MY BODY YOU, ENEMY, WILL NOT KILL ME." The models wore clothing reflecting the refugee experience. As one fashion critic reported, "the theme of rescue and dangerous crossings resonated through the tailored collection of sport T-shirts with invisible zippers, coats with inflatable vests, and transparent shirts and coats that rustled as the models moved."

Holzer has even projected words onto an ocean wave: at night on a Brazilian beach, "I SMILE." Of course, the phrase shows up only when a wave rolls in, and only for a moment, until the wave breaks. Its cheerful message flashes before you, then it's gone. Until the next wave. You have to watch and wait.

The fact that Holzer's works don't always appear in museums (although they have) doesn't mean they aren't as serious as any other kind of art. Holzer addresses the deepest personal and social issues. But she also admits, "I tend to gravitate to the most dreadful things—a good practice or a disability, I don't

Life message projected on a cliff in San Diego, California.

know which…. I am always sure that the sky is falling." And she is content to be anonymous in her work, to let it speak for itself: "I like to be out of view and out of earshot."

Today, at sixty-nine, Holzer continues to work at her home in Hoosick Falls and her studio in Brooklyn. She is a role model for creative thinking of any kind—in medicine, chemistry, technology, biology, and physics, as well as art and writing—where people make breakthroughs by ignoring what everyone else is doing and trying something completely new. Modestly summing up her work, she says, "I show what I can with words in light and motion in a chosen place, and when I envelop the time needed, the space around, the noise, smells, the people looking at one another and everything before them, I have given what I know."

Or, as one of her very own messages might put it, "THE SUM OF YOUR ACTIONS IS WHO YOU ARE."

Jenny Holzer smiles in front of her installation *Red Tilt* in the museum in Goslar, Germany.

14. UNBUILDABLE BUILDINGS?

Zaha Hadid, architect, Iraq (1950-2016)

Two hundred forty-three feet in the air, about the height of the Statue of Liberty, four construction workers sit at the top of the steel "space frame" of the futuristic new building Zaha Hadid has designed in Baku, Azerbaijan. The building is the Heydar Aliyev Cultural Center. They are waiting to bolt into place a seven hundred-pound concrete panel a crane is slowly lifting towards them. Neither a square nor a rectangle, it looks more like a giant guitar pick. It is just one of three thousand six hundred panels that will cover the frame to complete the structure.

From below come the sounds of cars and trucks on the streets of the eastern European capital. The panel swings back and forth in the wind, which is strong this afternoon, so the workers watch the panel carefully. They don't want it to slide into them, scraping them off the frame.

Zaha Hadid is the only woman ever to win the Pritzker Prize for the world's greatest living architect. She designed the Aliyev Center so the outer walls and roof flow together in one continuous surface, swooping high into the sky, then dropping all the way back to the ground before soaring right back up again. One observer describes the building as "a great floppy pancake," another as "the brim of a giant beach hat." The surface is smooth and white, looking like poured cream suddenly flash-frozen.

When construction manager Hannes Zimmerman first saw the plans, he said to himself, "This will never be built, because it looks like science fiction. Never, ever."

The panel finally swings close enough that the workers can guide it into place, sliding the holes in each

Pritzker Prize-winning architect Zaha Hadid.

The Heydar Aliyev Center, showing its remarkable contours and skin.

corner over matching bolts protruding from the frame. Once the crane settles the slab on the structure, the workers bolt it down. Unlike the bricks used on traditional buildings, each of the panels on this building is a unique shape and size. No two are the same.

The workers settle back, waiting for the next slab. Looking out over the city, they see a low, somber skyline. No building is taller than this one. No building has as bright a skin. It is the sign of a new era in Azerbaijan, reinventing itself after years of Soviet rule.

Hadid's buildings are so original and different they should be unbuildable. The amazing thing is, they're not. And they're spectacular to look at and fun to be in. Only one was unbuildable, but not because of its design.

* * *

Born in Baghdad on October 31, 1950, Zaha Hadid was the daughter of Iraqi parents. Her father was a business executive and politician, her mother an artist who regularly took Zaha to art museums. Hadid recalled, "I was a very curious child. I used to wander around all day asking questions. I had a fabulous childhood. But I was very shy. I think maybe by eleven years old I already wanted to become an architect. In my generation there were many women who wanted to become architects. It was not uncommon."

She loved visiting the ancient Sumerian cities of Iraq and credits the "fluid landscape" of the Middle East, its rivers, dunes, and wind-smoothed sandstone temples for the look and feel of her own curvy buildings. "The world is not a rectangle," she says. "You don't go into a park and say, 'My God, we don't have any corners.'"

As a teenager Zaha attended a boarding school in England. Afterwards, she entered the American University of Beirut, Lebanon as a math major. Hadid graduated in 1972 at twenty-two. She immediately enrolled at the Architectural Association in London because it was the most innovative school she could find. When she graduated in 1977, Professor Elia Zenghelis called her "the most outstanding pupil I ever taught." A dynamic presence even then, Hadid had a head of thick, curly auburn hair, dark eyebrows, a prominent nose, and a deep, throaty voice. Though deadly serious about her work, she also laughed a lot. She dressed fashionably, often with an edge, favoring deep reds and blacks.

In 1980, at thirty, she founded her very own architectural firm, Zaha Hadid Associates, in London. As her buildings rose around the world, from Azerbaijan to South Korea, from Spain to Cincinnati, Ohio, none of them looked the same. And none would have been possible without the sophisticated 3-D modeling programs Hadid developed. For while many architects used computers to perform basic calculations necessary to build structures, Hadid used them to design completely new kinds of buildings. Just as filmmakers used CGI (computer-generated imagery) to transform movies, Hadid used computers to transform architecture.

A fellow architect from England once described Hadid simply as "a superstar" of talent. However, success and fame were neither quick nor easy for her. Her one unbuildable building turned out to be one of her first. And the issue was not her design.

In 1994, when Hadid was forty-four, she won an international competition to design a 1,900 seat opera house for the city of Cardiff in Wales. The selection committee of the Cardiff Bay Opera Trust chose her over 267 other architects, many quite famous. Typically, Hadid's plan was unusual, a "crystal necklace" formed by a long building with narrow bands of windows bent around a central, taller cube holding the theater. The waterfront structure boasted spectacular views of Cardiff Bay. But local politicians refused to approve money to construct it. A headline in a local newspaper shrieked about the design, "It's awful… like a deconstructed pigsty." The Cardiff Bay Opera Trust ordered a second competition. Hadid won this and a third round, too. But the local Cardiff Council still thought her design "elitist" and radical. Labeling it "unbuildable," the Council awarded the commission to another, lesser architect, Jonathan Adams, a local man from a Cardiff architectural firm.

"It was such a depressing time," Hadid told reporter Rowan Moore. "I didn't look very depressed maybe but it was really dire. I made a conscious decision not to stop, but it could have gone the other way." An architect friend explained, "Cardiff in the late 1990's was not the place to try to build an adventurous piece of architecture, especially if you were an adventurous Arab and an adventurous woman architect."

Of prejudices, Hadid said later, "I have encountered them... in the Anglo-Saxon world—here in the U.K., maybe in America. I don't think that it was in any way hidden—[and] there was commentary by certain people in various papers, on the radio—maybe not because I'm a woman, but because I'm a foreigner." And, she might have added, from a Sunni Muslim family. "You cannot believe," she said to one interview, "the enormous resistance I've faced just for being an Arab, and a woman on top of that. It is like a double-edged sword. The moment my woman-ness is accepted, the Arab-ness seems to become a problem. I've broken beyond the barrier, but it's been a very long struggle. It's made me tougher and more precise—and maybe this is reflected in my architecture. I still experience resistance, but I think this keeps you on the go."

In the end, Hadid was able to use her

Central Theater of the Guangzhou Opera House, that might have been in Wales.

design for the opera house in Guangzhou, China, where residents were happy to have it. The opera house was unbuildable in Wales, yes, but not because of her design.

Completed in 2012, The Broad Art Museum at Michigan State is one of Hadid's most radical buildings. Constructed of stainless steel, with windows everywhere, the building has an entrance at a 45 degree angle. The museum's sides are parallelograms, not rectangles. No matter which way you look at the building, you think it's going to fall over. A professor of Hadid's once joked of her, "We called her the inventor of the 89 degrees. Nothing was ever at 90 degrees." But of course the Broad Museum hasn't fallen over. Inside, sunny walls of windows tilt over you thrillingly. Doors lean wittily left and right. You know you're somewhere different. And that's why you've come to an art museum, isn't it: to see creative work, imaginative work, different work, something you've never seen before?

Challenging your expectations, the Broad Museum dares you to enter.

One visitor says, "The building is ultra-modern, a perfect setting for a museum of modern art." But she also admits, "You get a slight feeling of vertigo when inside because of the architecture." A visitor with a contrary opinion writes on TripAdvisor: "Ugliest building on campus, looks like a collapsed pair of Venetian blinds destroyed by a cat." Differing opinions indeed, but the building is unarguably exciting. In 2016, filmmakers used it for a key scene in "Batman vs. Superman: Dawn of Justice."

The Aliyev Center was completed in 2012, the same year as the Broad Art Museum. The Center houses three different spaces in one building: a museum, a library, and an auditorium. Described by designer Danny Forster as requiring "one of the most complex roofing projects ever attempted," the Center has no columns or posts inside. It's all open. Yet although the roof looks floppy from the outside, it is anything but. The reinforced concrete panels the workers set in place by hand rest on the super strong steel web of the frame. Their one-of-a-kind shapes required calculations only a sophisticated computer could make— and which had never before been attempted. Harold Halvorsen, the project's roofing chief, reflected cheerfully, "Constructing the roof was a nightmare." Yet it stands strong.

Hadid said, "The idea was to make a completely seamless building, so the landscape literally crawls up the edge of the building and becomes like a mountain." Its developer, Tahir Gozel, loves the Center because he says that unlike

Sleek, smooth, and lit from within, the DDP appears
almost unearthly.

other tall buildings that make people feel small, this one inspires them. "The whole purpose is empowering the individual…. Being inside those curvatures, suddenly someone is struck and says, 'I can be this building. Wow. This is me.'"

Opened in 2014, the Dongdaemun Design Plaza in Seoul, the capital of South Korea, is the newest and most exciting building in the famous Dongdaemun fashion and shopping district. It opened when Hadid was sixty-four. The DDP, as it is known, houses state-of-the-art stores, a public library, and exhibition galleries. The largest free-form building in the world, it covers about three times the area of the average U. S. baseball stadium. Like the Aliyev Center, the DDP has no supporting columns, just forty-five thousand steel panels over a steel frame, more than ten times the number on the Aliyev Center.

From the outside at night, the DDP looks like nothing less than a saucer-shaped alien spaceship. Thousands of interior lights flicker in yellow patterns from the windows of its curvy glass and metal skin. The building looms four stories high, with three additional levels underground. Ramps and walkways beckon. Inside, the all-white floors and ceilings seem like decks on a cruise ship, but a cruise *space*ship. Visitors report feeling they could be lifted into outer space at any moment. People take photographs inside and out. But the size and complexity of the structure can also be daunting. One visitor notes, "The Dongdaemun Design Plaza is… a must-see for all architecture lovers. With a UFO exterior and Gaudi-esque interior, the building provides moments of beauty interspersed with extreme frustration when trying to navigate one's way around it."

Despite Hadid's enormous success, people continue to wonder why her buildings, which characteristically have no interior supports, few straight lines, and none of the usual building materials like bricks and beams, don't fall down. How can their roofs stay up without columns or posts? How can her roofs and walls undulate like waves or fabric when they are made out of heavy concrete and steel? The deep answer is what Hadid and her close collaborator Patrik Schumacher called "Parametricism," a design practice they invented themselves. "Parametric design," explains another architect, Pier Gough, "is fundamentally where you allow the computer—you feed it various ideas—and then you allow it to invent forms that you probably couldn't do in your mind. It's of such complexity that your brain couldn't think of it, and certainly your hand couldn't sketch it." Enabling fluid designs impossible to conceive before, the computer also produces the computations needed to actually execute them.

According to Hadid, when she started out, "I just wanted to do interesting work. And I cannot deny, I was very ambitious." Says one designer who worked with her, "Always there's a pressure for innovation." Hadid herself elaborated, "I know from my experience that without research and experimentation not much can be discovered. With experimentation, you think you're going to find out one thing, but you actually discover something else. That's what I think is really exciting. You discover much more than you bargain for. I think there should be no end to experimentation."

Eventually Hadid employed over four hundred associates at her architecture firm, working on projects in forty-four different countries. In addition to many honors, including the Pritzker Prize, in 2003 Hadid was honored by

Queen Elizabeth II, who made her a Dame of the British Empire, the female equivalent of a knight.

Throughout her life Hadid worked very hard. She admitted she was a demanding boss. But she enjoyed being and thinking differently. "I am eccentric, I admit it," she once laughed, "but I am not a nutcase."

Zaha Hadid died of a heart attack on March 31, 2016 in Miami, Florida at the age of 65. At one point in her life she was the highest paid architect in the world, with an estimated worth of over $200 million. She owned property around the world, several restaurants, and a soccer team. Cosmetics, perfume, a vodka brand, and a fashion line all bore her name. Her architecture firm and her work, of course, outlive her. Hadid's remarkable technical know-how, coupled with her imagination and daring—especially her daring—resulted in the creation of soaring structures that look more ready to take flight than to rest on the earth. They seem, in fact, to be from the distant future or outer space. As such, they cannot help but inspire us.

15. TOP ART COP—IN THE WORLD

Mireille Ballestrazzi, Art Detective and
President of INTERPOL, France (1954-   )

When five gunmen burst into the Marmottan art museum in Paris at 10:15 A.M. on the sunny Sunday morning of October 27, 1985, visitors soon found themselves on the floor, arms outspread.

About thirty tourists were enjoying the Impressionist paintings in the museum, formerly a millionaire's private home. "Everyone was on the floor, like in a bank," Yves Brayer, the museum's curator, said later. "This is the first time anyone has stolen paintings with weapons. One guard was trembling like a crazy man." The thieves put a gun to his head before locking him and the other seven guards in a closet.

Two of the intruders plunged into the galleries, hung with the colorful paintings people from around the world flocked to see. Among them was Claude Monet's painting *Impression, Sunrise*, which gave the Impressionist movement its name.

Impression, Sunrise, the painting that gave the Impressionists their name.

While three of the thieves covered the hostages, the other two removed nine paintings. Carrying them out to a double-parked car, they slid them into the trunk. The other three ran out, then they all sped away. Start to finish, less than five minutes.

Brayer estimated the works to be worth $12.5 million; others said $20 million. This may have been because of *Impression, Sunrise.* Four other Monets were taken, as well as works by Impressionists Pierre-Auguste Renoir and Berthe Morisot, and a painting by Japanese artist Sei-ichi Naruse.

Museum official Josette Tavera said of the thieves, "They were connoisseurs. They knew what they were looking for." Apparently they also knew the museum's alarms were switched off between 8:15 A.M. and 6 P.M.

"It's the theft of the century," lamented Brayer to the press. Why? Because of the value and popularity of the works. People love Impressionist paintings. They generally depict cheerful outdoor scenes like picnickers beside rivers, boaters on lakes, and families enjoying flower-filled fields under clear blue skies. Monet and the other Impressionists were ridiculed when they first exhibited their work because of the loose, free style of their brushstrokes. Critics said they didn't know how to paint. However, once it was understood they were not trying to make realistic images like those from a camera, but to portray the *feeling* of a scene, they won appreciation.

Police theorized that a radical group called Action Direct had pulled the job. The group had already carried out a number of high-profile robberies and even assassinations. Officials assumed Action Direct would demand a ransom for the return of the paintings. Certainly no one could sell them; the works were far too famous. But in the end there was no ransom demand. Action Direct never came forward. The case went cold.

Until an unusual participant got involved, a little-known art cop named Mireille Ballestrazzi. Still at work fighting crime today, Ballestrazzi has strong features, with a straight nose, sharp chin, wide-set brown

Art detective Mireille Ballestrazzi, the first female president of INTERPOL.

eyes, and a firm mouth that nonetheless warms quickly to a smile. Her dark hair is cut short and stylish. She wears fashionable clothes. Red is a favorite color. Married, Ballestrazzi has two grown children.

* * *

Born in 1954 in the village of Orange in the rural Vaucluse, to a military father and homemaker mother, Ballestrazzi lived in ten different cities as a child, as the army moved her father from one assignment to another. A ballet student from the age of five, Ballestrazzi soon switched to martial arts, specializing in judo and aikido. In high school in Lille, Mireille studied philosophy, mathematics, history, geography, and four languages: French, Latin, Greek, and English. She and her friends studied hard. Mireille said later, "These years were ideal preparation for my police job, where I also had to work nights and weekends." At university Mireille earned a Bachelor of Arts in Classics and a master's degree in Greek and Latin. She planned to be a professor. Then she read a magazine article her mother had cut out, announcing that for the first time ever, a few women would be allowed to take the national police exam.

Mireille, just twenty, immediately applied. Why did she suddenly switch paths? "I like adventure and responsibility" is her answer. A career in law enforcement seemed to offer both. But Mireille was turned away. You have to be twenty-one, she was told. So she waited a year, then reapplied. After a two-day written exam followed by an interview, Ballestrazzi won one of the four places open to women in the French Superior National Police Academy. Here her martial arts instructor nicknamed her "The Tigress" for the determination she showed in practice. She graduated in 1976 at twenty-two.

This was only the beginning of a remarkable law enforcement career. Just two years later, in 1978, Ballestrazzi became Head of the Organized Crime division of the region of Bordeaux, to the south of Paris. In 1985, the year of the Marmottan heist, she was head of the Judicial Police in the city of Argenteuil. But in July, 1987 at thirty-three years old, Ballestrazzi became chief of the Central Office for the Suppression of Art Theft in Paris, and the Marmottan case grew hot again. It happened accidentally, when Ballestrazzi investigated another major case of art theft she hadn't even known about when she came to Paris.

On October 19, 1984, three years before Ballestrazzi's arrival in Paris, thieves broke into a quiet little museum in the quiet little village of Semur-en-Auxois, known for its picturesque medieval towers. With the low crime rate in the rural area, the museum's security was minimal. Unfortunately, the loss was not. Thieves

Semur-en-Auxois.

took five paintings by Jean-Baptiste Corot, a popular French landscape paint-er. He specialized in country scenes peopled by farmers, shepherds, and milk-maids. Corot's work was known as "the most faked art in the world" because so many art forgers made copies of his scenes to sell to unsuspecting collectors. The five stolen paintings were *Evening, The Orchard, Sunset, Boy Wearing a Cap,* and *Portrait of Mme. Baudot.*

Evening was a particularly beloved scene of a country twilight, with feath-ery trees against a rosy sunset and a farm couple, tiny in the darkening land-scape, walking home. Ballestrazzi had been in Paris for only three months when police in Tokyo, Japan called. They'd arrested a self-described "art dealer" who was taking *Evening* from art gallery to art gallery trying to sell it. Was she in-terested?

Of course the Tigress was interested. Ballestrazzi immediately gathered a team of five investigators. Arriving at Haneda Airport after a nineteen-hour flight, she and her team found themselves facing a mob of two hundred jour-nalists. The Japanese couldn't imagine a woman in such an important leader-ship position as a police commissioner. Reporters peppered here with all sorts of questions. Ballestrazzi kept a straight face and answered calmly. They nick-named her "the ice doll."

The man offering *Evening* turned out to be forty-seven year-old Shinichi Fujikuma, a member of Japan's *yazuka,* a crime syndicate like the Italian mafia.

Some years earlier, Ballestrazzi learned, Fujikuma had been jailed in France for heroin trafficking. While behind bars he'd met two Frenchmen, Phillipe Jamin, thirty-one, and Youssef Khimoun, thirty-three, who specialized in art thefts. Together they'd planned the theft of the Corots.

Corot painted several paintings titled *Evening*.
Here is one from the Art Gallery of South Australia.

Jamin and Khimoun smuggled the paintings into Japan some years later. They picked Japan because it had an especially short statute of limitations for stolen art. The statute of limitations is the length of time after a crime during which criminals may still be charged and prosecuted. After the statute of limitations runs out, the criminals are safe from prosecution. In Japan, for stolen art, that was just two years. And while buyers in the West demanded backup documentation for art works, Japanese collectors weren't so particular. Fujikuma sold the Corots to several businessmen. But when Ballestrazzi and the Tokyo police confronted these men, they refused to give back the paintings. They claimed they had bought them on good faith. They didn't know they were stolen. Ballestrazzi and her team didn't believe them, but she couldn't prove they were lying. And she couldn't legally prosecute them because two years had passed.

Finally Ballestrazzi insisted, "I'm not leaving without the paintings." The Japanese government stepped in, pressuring the men. Eventually, they returned the works, all except one. The owner of *Portrait of Mme. Baudot* claimed he had put too much money into restoring it to return it. So *Mme. Baudot* is still in Japan, illegally.

Jamin and Khimoun, Fujikuma's accomplices, were nowhere to be found. All the Tokyo police knew was that they had flown to Singapore on the night of November 25, 1986, the day of the largest armed robbery in Japanese history. Thieves wearing masks and wielding toy guns and Mace stole $2.4 million from a Mitsubishi Bank armored car in central Tokyo. Just like the heist of the Monets at the Marmottan Museum, it all happened in broad daylight.

Returning to Paris with her team and four Corot paintings, Ballestrazzi recalls, "When we touched down at Roissy [airport] I was happy to have justified the confidence placed in me, happy to return the Corots to France, but above all happy to return to my family." She meant her husband Christian and her children, ages two and four at the time.

The return of the high-profile art works brought Ballestrazzi her first public recognition. It is rare for stolen art to be recovered, especially from another country and undamaged. Only about ten percent of stolen art works ever come back, in any condition, despite the fact that some fifty to a hundred thousand items are stolen every year.

The case gave Ballestrazzi a unique international perspective. As she said, "The time I spent as head of this [Paris] bureau showed me how efficient collaborations with foreign police services and the assistance of INTERPOL can be." The trip also ended up leading to the Monets stolen at the Marmottan.

In Fujikuma's Tokyo apartment Ballestrazzi had found a catalog from the Marmottan. Circled in ink were nine paintings, the same ones stolen in the holdup. Ballestrazzi and Fujikuma had a conversation. While Fujikuma never confessed to the heist, he did tell her that the Monets turned out to be unsellable, even to Japanese buyers. The paintings were just too well known for anyone to be caught with them. Plus, the paintings had been taken in an armed holdup. One Japanese collector had been interested, no questions asked, but he never closed the deal.

Fujikuma's information led Ballestrazzi to believe the paintings might never have left France for Japan, so she began a quiet investigation in her own country. Its direction was based on a letter she had seen on her trip to Tokyo, suggesting that one of the intermediaries in the Corot affair was a martial arts instructor from Corsica. An island just off the French and Italian coasts, Corsica was the birthplace of Napoleon. Well known for their love of independence, its inhabitants had a particular lack of interest in any kind of investigators from the mainland.

An ancient tower guards the secretive island of Corsica.

After three years of secret, persistent detective work, Ballestrazzi believed she could identify a Corsican crime circle of about thirty men. Over four days, December 2-5, 1990, she directed the secret infiltration of thirty special police officers, including herself, onto the island. Ballestrazzi used four different airports (Figari, Calvi, Bastia, and Ajaccio) to avoid arousing suspicion. On December 5, in a night raid at several locations at once, officers bursting through doors arrested fifteen suspects.

In the home of thirty year-old Pierre Donatien Comiti, Ballestrazzi's team found photographs of the stolen works. At 3 A.M. that morning, an interrogator called Ballestrazzi to say Comiti had confessed. At 6 A.M., Comiti led Ballestrazzi and members of her team to an unoccupied villa in the quiet seaside town of Porto Vecchio. Entering, they found all nine missing paintings in a large wooden crate. Fortunately only two were damaged. Berthe Morisot's *Young Girl at the Ball* had two holes. Monet's own *Field of Tulips, Holland* suffered a tear. The thieves hadn't been careful, but at least they hadn't been purposely destructive. *Impression, Sunrise* was untouched.

Berthe Morisot's slightly damaged *Young Girl at the Ball*.

In a France 2 TV press conference in Paris on December 6, Marmottan curator Armand d'Hauterives, said, "It's the best Christmas present we could have." Ballestrazzi explained,

"We could have acted sooner, but we wanted to ensure none of the paintings would be destroyed." She was well aware that with art thefts, it's all about the safe return of the works. The greatest worry is that thieves will destroy them to eliminate the evidence of their wrongdoing. With art crime, arresting the guilty is always secondary.

Comiti claimed he was just acting on behalf of others, and was not one of the actual thieves. Ballestrazzi turned him over for prosecution, but released

Ballestrazzi and her team display the valuable art they
recovered in their daring raid.

the others. It turned out that the works had been hidden on the island for five years. They were just too, too hot for anyone.

Ballestrazzi revealed that tracking telephone calls between Japan and Corsica had been key. She also said that the perpetrators were "ordinary criminals," not members of an organized crime syndicate or political group. Apparently Shinichi Fujikuma enlisted Philippe Jamin and Youssef Khimoun for the Marmottan job after their success with the Corots. In 1988 Jamin was arrested in Mexico in conjunction with the Tokyo hold-up. He received a six-year sentence, but he was never charged in the Marmottan theft. Khimoun remains at large.

France bestowed on Ballestrazzi its highest civilian award, Commander of the Legion of Honor. On November 8, 2012, she received an historic international honor when she was elected president of INTERPOL (International Criminal Police Organization), the world's police force. She was the first woman ever to hold the office. INTERPOL has one hundred ninety member countries. The second largest international organization in the world after the United Nations, its police forces cooperate in fighting drug and human trafficking, terrorism, wildlife and environmental crimes, tech crime, art theft, weapons smuggling, and a host of other illegal activities. Its passport database facilitates screening checks at airports and border crossings all over the world.

Interviewed after the INTERPOL appointment, Ballestrazzi said, "Of course I am happy they have put their trust in me. I am proud for women because this can have an impact and I am proud for France." She also noted that crime, especially drug dealing and human trafficking, has become increasingly international. On Ballestrazzi's list of priorities for INTERPOL were stopping the illegal trade of rare woods and rhinoceros horns from Africa, halting corruption in sports, and curtailing international cybercrime.

Ballestrazzi served a four-year term, stepping down from the position in 2016 at age sixty-two.

The Sunday morning theft at the Marmottan is the most publicized crime challenge that Ballestrazzi ever faced. Through perseverance the Tigress found her way to a little-known village in Corsica and the safe return of some of France's most valuable national treasures. As a young woman Mireille Ballestrazzi said she wanted a job with "adventure and responsibility." She got her wish. She experienced both at the highest level, as the world's top cop.

16. A STUDENT SCHOOLS THEM ALL

Maya Lin, Architect, USA (1959-   )

I t all began with mashed potatoes, when Maya Lin was a Yale senior, twenty-one years old. It ended up as a national memorial in Washington, DC. How on earth?

Maya Lin lived in Saybrook College, one of the gray stone dormitories on quadrangles of green lawns where students sunned and studied in good weather. One cold winter evening in 1981, she paused in the cafeteria line of the college dining room and loaded up the blue china plate on her tray with mashed potatoes. Lots of them. Piling on more than she could possibly eat, she ignored the astonished stares of the servers in white coats and hairnets standing behind the steaming tubs of food. Usually it was the six-foot-five crew jocks who loaded up their plates, not slender architecture students. But Lin didn't really care what they thought. Lin had an idea, and no one was going to stop her. Scoop after scoop she took, until she had about three pounds piled up.

Then she carried her plate into the dining room and over to a table, sitting down alone. The room was almost as grand as the Great Hall at Hogwarts. A vaulted ceiling rose high above lines of long oak tables. On the walls, portraits of distinguished former professors, all men in black academic robes or dark suits, stared down. The smell of hot food from the serving line mingled with the voices of young men and women at the tables beside her.

Lin didn't eat the potatoes. Well, maybe one or two mouthfuls. Instead, she started pushing the potatoes around with a spoon, a knife, and her fingers.

A slim young woman with straight black hair to her waist, a round face, deep brown eyes, and a small mouth that easily broke into a mischievous grin, Lin liked being active. She often roller-skated on the stone plaza in front of the august Beinecke Library, just for fun. Now, mushing and squishing, prodding and pushing, Lin scooped out a broad, shallow triangle in the mound of potatoes. The sides of the triangle were two "walls" of potatoes. Meeting, they formed an inverted V.

Lin was making a model for a project in her class on funerary architecture. That is, tombs, mausoleums, memorials, and cemeteries. While many people think architects design just buildings, in fact they design all sorts of things. The Vietnam War had ended just five years before, and a call had gone out from Washington for artists, sculptors, and architects to submit designs for a memorial to those who had died or gone missing. Lin recalled, "One of us, I can't remember who, found a poster that advertised a competition for the Vietnam Veterans Memorial, and we said, what a great idea! Let's make that our final project for this course!" Lin was imagining the potatoes were mounds of earth on The Mall in Washington, D.C., the long park that stretches all the way from the Capitol to the Washington Monument.

* * *

Maya Lin was born on October 5, 1959 in Athens, Ohio. Her parents had emigrated from China after the communists under Mao Zedong took over in the late 1940s. Of her mother Lin says, "She got smuggled out on a junk boat in Shanghai Harbor when the harbor was being bombed in 1949... My mother at the age of 18 or 17 never saw her father again. She was so close to him. To this day, I'll remember when she got the letter that he had passed away. And she just was—and—you know, you never think about it when you're that age."

The quiet, serious co-valedictorian of her high school class in Athens, Lin was the only Asian student in her grade. She wore her straight black hair long, ignoring makeup. Lin made her own clothes, preferring them to store-bought. She enjoyed hiking, reading, and especially hanging out in her father's studio.

Cherry trees in
Assistens Kirkegård cemetery.

A ceramicist, he was also Dean of the College of Fine Arts at Ohio University in Athens. "I literally had the whole art school to play in as a kid," Lin remembers. Her mother, a poet, taught literature at the university.

During her junior year at Yale, Lin traveled to Denmark for a semester abroad. There she was fascinated by a huge, beautiful cemetery that often had as many living people in it as those buried or entombed. To her, a cemetery and a memorial weren't that different. Both were places for the living to remember, honor, and relate to the dead. In the U.S. and other countries, people rarely visit cemeteries. But the Danes used Assistens Kirkegård cemetery in Copenhagen as a park. People came all the time. They brought books, picnics, friends, and their families.

Assistens Kirkegård boasts long allées of tall, skinny poplars, shrubs of all kinds, gravel paths, flowering trees, and broad lawns. When Lin visited, she might have seen two women sitting on the grass sharing take-out coffees, joggers in T-shirts passing by, teens playing soccer. Hans Christian Andersen, author of "The Little Mermaid," "The Ugly Duckling," and many other stories, is buried there. "I wasn't fascinated with death," Lin says. "It was just from an architectural point of view. It was interesting." And a way for the living and the dead to share a beautiful space.

So when she returned to Yale, Lin "got together with eleven other students and we decided to set up our own course that would deal with funerary architecture." They convinced Professor Andrus Burr to teach them. All that was behind the potatoes. The project was a course requirement, to be sure. But it was also something more to Lin, an opportunity to design a site in nature.

"My work is always about the environment," she says. "I think what my work is about is appreciating and being respectful of nature, which again ties in to an inherent love for the natural environment.... I know that nothing I do can ever be better than what this planet, what this land, what the natural resources, what this place is."

An organization called the Vietnam Veterans Memorial Fund (VVMF), founded by former Army corporal Jan C. Scruggs, was sponsoring the competition. There were four stipulations. The memorial had to be reflective and contemplative in character; harmonize with its surroundings; contain the names of all who died or remained missing; and make no political statement about the war.

Traditionally, war memorials feature statues of soldiers with weapons, always men. The General Sherman Memorial at Grand Army Plaza in New York City is an officer riding a horse, a sword strapped to his thigh. The Audie Murphy War Memorial in Greenville, Texas, shows a World War II infantryman brandishing a machine gun. The Minuteman statue in Lexington, Massachusetts is a bareheaded man holding a rifle.

Instead, Lin wanted to use the earth at the site itself. She imagined it embracing the names of all the soldiers who had given their lives or gone missing, the women as well as men. She wanted the spot to look and be beautiful, too. The requirement about the names really spoke to Lin. She regularly passed through the Memorial Rotunda of Woolsey Hall on the way to classes. The names of Yale graduates who died in American wars, from the Revolution to the present, were recorded on white marble walls there. Lin would stop and run her fingers over the names. They seemed to speak to her personally, as individuals. As a freshman she stopped to watch workmen carefully incising the names of those who had died so recently in the Vietnam War itself. Each person's name, year of graduation, branch of service, and date and place of death were included. For example: "David Webster, 1951, Major, U.S.M.C., March 10, 1963, Vietnam."

Lin had also seen slides of British architect Sir Edwin Lutyens' Memorial to the Missing at Somme, in Thiepval, France. It was a giant triple arch inscribed with the names of 72,246 British soldiers killed in World War I whose bodies were never found or could not be identified. The Memorial overlooks a cemetery of crosses and tombstones beneath which lie the remains of six hundred soldiers, but it was the names and the number of them that struck Lin. Lin wanted her memorial to offer some sort of personal encounter with the individuals who had died, just as she felt with the soldiers in Woolsey Hall.

Soon after her evening with the potatoes, Lin made a proper model out of clay in her studio in the massive seven-story "A and A" (Art and Architecture) Building at Yale. This model showed two walls, each to be 246 feet long, out of polished black granite. Descending into the earth to a point ten feet below ground level, they met to make a 125-degree V. On the walls: the names of 58,276 American men and women. The end of one wall pointed to the Washington monument, the other to the Lincoln Memorial, to create "a unity between the nation's past and present," as Lin put it. No statues. No weapons. The walls and slope should draw visitors into the memorial itself, down to its heart.

Lin walked the proposed site of the memorial in November, with classmates on the way back from Thanksgiving vacation. It was then just an empty bit of park with unmowed grass and clumps of leafless trees. Some teenagers tossed a Frisbee. Lin remembers, "We went to visit the site, and I guess I just imagined

Maya Lin with her eventual full model of her design for
the Vietnam Veterans Memorial in Washington, D.C..

taking a knife, cutting open the earth, opening it up, an initial violence and pain that in time would heal...." She imagined visitors walking down into the memorial, scooped out of the earth itself.

Lin also made a drawing of the scene using blue and green pastels. The drawing was not a course requirement. She was actually going to send her design to Washington, formally entering the VVMF competition, as well as turning the project in to Prof. Andrus. The VVMF didn't require a model, but it did insist on a drawing and a statement explaining the idea behind the design.

As it turned out, Lin was the only one in her class who actually sent in a design (besides her professor). And she only just got it finished before the March 31 deadline. For Lin, the hardest part was writing the statement. That took her two whole months. Its conclusion emphasized that "this memorial is meant not as a monument to the individual, but rather as a memorial to the men and women who died during the war, as a whole.... Brought to a sharp awareness of such a loss, it is up to each individual to resolve or come to terms with this loss. For death is in the end a personal and private matter, and the area contained within this memorial is a quiet place meant for personal reflection and private reckoning."

Lin got her materials to the post office with just hours to spare. Besides the drawing and her statement, there was only a sealed envelope with her name inside. To make the competition absolutely fair, all entries had to be anonymous. The judging was to be absolutely unbiased. No one was to know who had done which design until the results were revealed on May 1, four weeks away.

Architecture was not even Lin's first choice for a profession. She entered Yale planning to become a zoologist. As a child, Lin said, "I wanted to be an animal behaviorist. I wanted to be a vet...so I would feed all of the raccoons.

I would feed the birds. The birds had me well trained. The red cardinal would come to the window and chirp knowing it was dinnertime, and I'd always be feeding them.... I would sit still in the yard trying to tame this one rabbit. And I got so close to this rabbit at the end that I could've touched it." However, when her faculty advisor at Yale, Professor Robert Apfel, explained that as a zoology student she'd have to perform vivisections, dissecting live animals, she changed her major to architecture. She really didn't mind. She saw architecture as a combination of art, science, and math, all three of which she liked.

Still, for a woman it was a field with challenges. Even now only eighteen percent of architects in the United States are female. Only one woman, Zaha Hadid, has ever won the Pritzker Prize, awarded each year to the world's greatest living architect. But Lin never minded challenges. She was strong that way.

While Lin continued classes at Yale, finishing her senior year, her envelope arrived at VVMF headquarters in Washington along with one thousand four hundred twenty others, from all over the world. Lin's entry was No. 1026.

The jury to pick the winning design included two sculptors, two architects, two landscape architects, and one humanist. Four were veterans. All were men. Because there were so many entries, the VVMF hung them on panels in Hanger 3 at Andrews Air Force Base in Maryland, a cavernous space capable of sheltering huge cargo planes and bombers. The members of the jury spent several days strolling through the hangar examining the entries. Their first cut reduced the number to two hundred thirty-two. Their second cut narrowed their choices to thirty-nine. Finally they found themselves gathered around No.1026.

Everyone knew a professional, adult architect in the male-dominated profession would win the commission to actually build the memorial. It was of national importance, after all. It would stand forever in the heart of the nation's capital, on "America's front lawn," just blocks from the Lincoln Memorial and Washington Monument and across the Tidal Basin from the Jefferson Memorial. The Lincoln was the work of a famous male sculptor, Daniel Chester French. The Jefferson was by another well-known man, the architect John Russell Pope.

The jurors' decision was unanimous: No.1026. Some of their comments were: "Totally eloquent." "Reverential." "He knows what's he's doing, all right."

On Friday, May 1, 1981, Jan Scruggs, flanked by fellow VVMF officials Robert Doubek and Jack

Aerial view of the Memorial showing V shape leading to apex at the deepest part.

Wheeler, announced the winner to a select gathering of veterans. As Scruggs later wrote, "The vets had expected that the winner would be a prominent professional working with a prestigious firm. Doubek looked up Number 1026. 'Maya Ying Lin.' An Asian name. She was 21 years old. She lived in New Haven, Connecticut. Wheeler recognized the address. An undergraduate residence at Yale." Everyone was, of course, astonished. But everyone on the jury, and the veterans hearing the announcement as well, loved the design.

Back at Yale, the May sun warmed the grass on the quadrangles between Yale's old stone buildings. Students spread blankets and lay on the grass, holding books. Studying for exams, some found it hard to keep their eyes open, sluggish with spring fever. As a college senior, with many things to think about, Lin let the competition slip from mind. Lin had had no real expectation that her entry would be noticed. She was just a student. And a woman.

On the very last day of school, Lin was in class when her roommate Liz Perry suddenly appeared at the door, frantically signaling. When Lin finally saw her, she tiptoed out. Perry said some people from Washington had called. They wanted to ask her some questions about her entry. The callers were from the VVMF. They wanted to fly up to New Haven to meet with her. Of course, Lin agreed, but not with any particular excitement. Lin recalls, "I was convinced that I was number 100 and they were only going to question me about drainage and other technical issues...."

But the next day three men in suits arrived, sitting down with Lin in her cramped dormitory suite. A former Marine colonel, Donald Schaet, guided the conversation. Recalling this most unusual meeting, Lin says, "Even after Colonel Schaet, who was talking, without missing a beat calmly added that I had won (I think my roommate's face showed more emotion than mine did at the time), it still hadn't registered. I don't think it did for almost a year."

Out of one thousand four hundred twenty-one entries by some of the most distinguished architects and designers in the world, Maya Ying Lin, unknown student from Yale, was the winner. (In the course Prof. Burr gave her a B- for her design, a C+ overall.)

How could Lin not be flabbergasted? You draw something, you make a model, you show it, as if at a middle school science fair, and then people say, "We're actually going to build it!" In the middle of the nation's capital, no less.

On the afternoon Lin graduated, she drove straight to Washington for the official announcement and press conference. In the glare of bright lights, with TV cameras tracking her, Maya stood at a podium bristling with microphones, as Scruggs introduced her. Smiling broadly, he announced, "Some of the finest artists and architects in the country and some of the highest-priced firms did enter this competition, and they all lost." Lin giggled. A reporter asked, "Are your parents here?" "Yes," she answered happily. "They're right back there." She pointed. "And my roommate." Beaming, she tipped her presentation board forward so everyone could see the model. Suddenly famous across the country and indeed around the world, she explained her design.

But Lin's joy was short-lived.

A reporter suddenly challenged: "'Isn't it ironic that the war in Vietnam was in Asia and you are of Asian descent?' Lin recalls, "I thought the question was completely racist…and completely irrelevant. I was as American as anyone else."

A letter arrived at VVMF headquarters asking, "How can you let a gook design the memorial?"

A wealthy businessman and later presidential candidate, H. Ross Perot, called her an "egg roll."

A senator, James Webb of Virginia, called Lin's design "a nihilistic slab."

A veteran, Tom Carhart, called it "an open urinal" and wrote in the *New York Times* that it was "a black gash of shame and sorrow."

A writer for *National Review* magazine, in an article titled "Stop That Monument," wrote "Okay, we lost the Vietnam War. Okay, the thing was mismanaged from start to finish. But the American soldiers who died in Vietnam fought for their country and for the freedom of others and they deserve better than the outrage that has been approved as their memorial…."

Lin, still only twenty-one, just graduated from college, was devastated. "I grew up in a college town in the middle of Appalachia," she explained, "so I'm still wearing Frye boots, and wearing my hair really long, and everyone's thinking I'm some sixties hippie. I have no idea what that's about. I'm not cutting my hair because I'm a good Chinese daughter. I'm wearing Frye boots because I'm a fashion disaster. And they connected me with antiwar and sixties radicals."

Lin hung in, trying to ignore the voices. What on earth had she done to earn such a reaction? Why did so many people seem to hate the memorial and her? Lin had won legitimately, but now, would her memorial even get built? The VVMF continued to back her. Her friends and family supported her. Still, what should have been a gloriously happy experience became a nightmare.

The problem wasn't Lin. It was her country's. The Vietnam War had torn the nation apart. Usually, young Americans uncomplainingly volunteered to fight. They did so in World Wars I and II. But in the Vietnam War U.S. soldiers began dying in large numbers without victory in sight. Numbers of Americans questioned their country's involvement. Many college students who were being drafted into the Armed Forces objected. Others joined mass protests. In a march on the Pentagon, college students famously poked daisies into the gun barrels of soldiers.

The Vietnam Veterans Memorial had to satisfy both those for and against the war.

And Lin's idea was so different from the usual memorial with statues of soldiers in heroic poses with weapons.

Lin took a small apartment in Washington with friends. She endured hours of debate in front of panels of politicians and experts. So many government agencies had to review so many details. The Commission of Fine Arts had to approve the design itself. The National Capital Planning Commission had to make sure it fit in with all the other monuments. The National Park Service controlled the plot of land it would be built on. The list went on and on.

And the opposition only grew stronger and nastier.

One critic thought that having polished walls was "too feminine." Another objected to the color of the walls. Lin recalls, "It took a prominent four-star general, Brigadier General George Price, who happened to be African-American...defending the color black, before the design could move forward." She recalls the officer "getting up in front of one of the subcommittee hearings and saying, 'I see nothing wrong with the color black.'" James Watt, Secretary of the Department of the Interior, which is responsible for the management of all federal lands and natural resources, had the ultimate authority. Calling a press conference, he announced that he just plain refused to issue a permit to start construction of the memorial.

The Commission of Fine Arts came under pressure to add a statue to Lin's design. At the hearing the media piled in with TV cameras, crowds of photographers and reporters, and the usual bright lights. Over three hundred members of the public filled two dozen rows of chairs. While Lin sat quietly in the back of the hot, close room, one opponent after another took to the podium to insist on their new idea: a bronze statue of three infantrymen. Featuring one Caucasian, one African-American, and one Hispanic solider, all male, all carrying weapons, the statue would stand at the center of Lin's V. Frederick Hart, the sculptor, had come in third in the VVMF competition. He told Lin, "My sculpture will improve your work." Lin was appalled. "As an artist, you should know to respect another person's art. I would never in a million years disrespect another artist that way."

But Lin never wilted. When it was finally her turn to speak, she strode to the front of the room in the pale blue dress and matching broad-brimmed hat she had of course made herself. Looking straight out at the crowd, the cameras, and the media, she responded in a clear, firm voice. She didn't betray the anger and hurt she was really feeling. Her design, she explained, "is not a memorial to politics or war or controversy but to all those men and women who served...." Pausing to let this point sink in, she continued, "I am not approving or disapproving of the sculpture per se. I disapprove of the forced melding of these two memorials into one." Lin spoke just a few words, she was calm, but she ceded no ground. Someone else's opinion wasn't going to stop her if she thought she was right.

Lin's rebuttal had an effect. The committee gave in, but not completely. Yes, the soldiers could be included. But they were to be placed one hundred fifty feet away from Lin's memorial. "Three Fighting Men" would have to be smaller, and they would have to be oriented so they looked at her design. Hart was paid $330,000 for his group. Lin received just $20,000, the award for first prize in the competition.

With her design finally approved, Lin left Washington, emotionally worn out, disappointed, disgusted. She didn't even return to see the first shovels go into the ground. She later said of the whole experience, "It took me a few years to recover from it." Not until cranes were lifting the engraved panels into place could she bring herself to return to the city.

But she remained strong. Back at Yale, one of her professors, Prof. Vincent Scully said, "Imagine standing up to all that. The word for Lin is 'courage.'" Lin proudly described herself as "stubborn." As she cheerfully told PBS interviewer Bill Moyers, ".... When you're so young, what do you have going for you? Total belief in what you've done. There was no doubt. As you get older, we all begin to have doubts. I think when you're twenty years old, you're right. And I knew I was right and once it was up, they would get it."

When Lin did return to Washington, it was for the official opening on November 13, 1982. She was twenty-three now. A bitter wind raking the Mall did not stop one hundred fifty thousand veterans, friends, supporters, and families from flocking to the site from all over the country.

Scruggs remembered a few stories of vets traveling to get there:

"A vet whose twin brother had died in Vietnam walked 1,255 miles to Washington.

"A vet hitchhiking to Washington fell asleep and awoke at the airport with a paid round-trip ticket in his pocket.

"A group of vets checked out of a VA hospital, penniless. A Congressional Medal of Honor winner took out a personal loan to rent a bus for them.

"All across America, such buses—along with airplanes and car caravans—became rolling barracks, as the men drifted into Washington from Boston, Cleveland, Dallas, Denver, and San Francisco; and from Stroud, Oklahoma; Fergus Falls, Minnesota; Jessup, Iowa; Bethel,

As visitors descend into the Memorial, the walls and names enclose them.

Connecticut; and all the other towns and cities whose sons had served. 'It was,' a newspaper in Beaumont, Texas, noted, 'as if they were all drawn by the same ghostly bugle.'"

A magazine reporter wrote, "Though the new monument designed by Maya Ying Lin had been deeply scorned by those who thought its starkness and subtlety shamed the veterans, many who viewed it were deeply moved. Soldiers walked over from the Pentagon in uniform. Parents of the war dead came, hand in hand. Some prayed, some cried, some knelt to kiss the name of a lost relative or combat buddy." The names include eight women, all nurses: seven from the Army, one from the Air Force.

Despite all the controversy, the Memorial was a success beyond Lin's and the VVMF's wildest dreams. Solemn, dignified, inclusive, it had a powerful effect. People touched the names and wept. They made rubbings to take home with them. They left teddy bears and flowers and photographs. And Lin got to stand there and see that it worked.

Lin once wrote, "I like to think of my work as creating a private conversation with each person, no matter how public each work is and no matter how many people are present." When Lin finally walked away that day, disappearing alone down the Mall, she left thousands still held by her memorial, having those conversations. And they continue to this day. The experience is so much like that of Lin's Danish inspiration, Assistens Kirkegård in Copenhagen, where

Veterans seek the names of friends and comrades.

the living meet with the dead. "The cost of war is in these individuals," Lin once said of the names, "and we have to remember them first."

The daughter of immigrants created a lasting, comforting memorial for American men and women in a troubled time of war. Today the wall hosts close to four million visitors a year. Veterans in uniform or old pieces of uniform cry and hug. As Scruggs observed, "On some days, over 20,000 people come. Late at night, at dawn, someone is always there." People touch the names of loved ones and weep. "As you read a name," Lin has said, "or touch a name, the pain will come out, and I really did mean for people to cry.... You have to accept and admit that this pain has occurred, in order for it to be healed."

In 2002, at age forty-three, Lin became the first Asian American selected to the Yale Corporation. Among many other honors, in 2016 she received the Presidential Medal of Freedom, the nation's highest civilian award, from

President Obama at the White House. He remarked, "When an undergraduate from rural Appalachia first set foot on the National Mall many years ago, she was trying to figure out a way to show that war is not just a victory or a loss, but about individual lives."

Today, age sixty, Lin lives in New York City with husband Daniel Wolf, a photography dealer. She has two daughters, India and Rachel. Lin oversees

President Barack Obama bestows the Presidential Medal of Freedom on Maya Lin.

a thriving practice, the Lin Studio, considering herself more a designer than an architect. Perhaps this is because she likes to create so many different works of art. In 1995 Lin created "Wave Field" for the University of Michigan, an outdoor landscape of undulating mounds of grass. She designed the granite "Women's Table," also outdoors, which carries the names of women at Yale from 1869 to 1993, when the table was installed. In 2009 Lin was the author of a new building for the Museum of Chinese in America in New York City. These are just

Maya Lin today, with models and drawings.

some of the numerous structures, sculptures, and landscape designs she has originated. A recent project, "A River in New York is a Drawing," is a study of the Hudson River, NY in various mediums, including maps, paintings, bamboo stakes, stainless steel "pin sculptures," and "streams" of pale green marbles winding over the Hudson River Museum's floors, walls, and ceilings.

Lin says, "My work has always been about finding art in the natural world." So it is now, so it was in her first public piece, the Vietnam Veterans Memorial.

Gertrude Gerber, a volunteer at Lin's memorial, clearly recognizes its power. There is a small shed Gertrude can step into when the weather is bad. She recalls, "We had a severe rainstorm the other day and I took shelter in the kiosk. This man and woman came up drenched to the skin and said they had a son killed in Vietnam and could I help them find his name. I invited them to step under the shelter and wait out the rain, but they refused. They went back to the wall and just stood there in the soaking rain staring at their son's name."

Maya Lin, a college student starting with a few scoops of mashed potatoes and remarkable determination, reached across gulfs of pain to touch millions.

17. CODA: "MASKED AVENGERS"

The Guerrilla Girls, activists, USA (1985-   )

This time they would be successful. This time they would get their message across. This time, people would pay attention!

As each of the young women who had gathered in the basement studio in lower New York City slipped on a stuffy, rubbery, stinky gorilla mask, she felt a special thrill. Wearing the mask she'd just bought at a costume store, each woman was suddenly more than just her name. Now she was a powerful beast, part of a wild, gorgeous tribe. Now she was a good bit scary. Now she was a Guerrilla Girl.

No, not that kind of gorilla, that lives in a rainforest in Rwanda. The other kind: *guerrilla*, a fighter for a cause who pops up from time to time, then fades away to fight another day. Nimble. Hard to catch. Even if it was hard to see out of the eye holes.

Some of them snatched up the posters they had made. Others picked up the pots of paste they needed to stick up the posters. Still others seized the extra-big brushes. Then they were out the door, onto the midnight streets of Greenwich Village and SoHo (South of Houston Street), two of the hottest arts districts in the city. They were going to plaster them with their posters. This time, their messages would not be ignored.

Who were they? Who are they? As they say on their website, "The Guerrilla Girls are feminist activist artists. We wear gorilla masks in public and use facts, humor, and outrageous visuals to expose gender and ethnic bias as well as corruption in politics, art, film, and pop culture."

Yes, but who were they? What were their real names? They won't say. They never say. "Our anonymity keeps the focus on the issues, and away from who we might be: we could be anyone."

The night of the Guerrilla Girls' first poster raid, there was still some traffic on the streets, despite the late hour. A few people were out, on their way home after work or a late dinner at a bistro. Overhead, stars winked between skyscrapers. An impatient taxi driver honked. A city bus growled, accelerating at a light. The Guerrilla Girls stopped first at a brick wall, empty except for other tattered posters. Slap, slap with the brush and paste. Up went the first two posters, stark, simple, attention-getting, just bold black type on a white background.

The first: "Women in America earn only 2/3 of what men do. Women artists earn only 1/3 of what men artists do." (Picture of a dollar bill sliced into thirds.)

The second: "How many women had one-person exhibitions at NYC museums last year?" (Answer: Guggenheim 0, Metropolitan 0, Modern 1, Whitney 0.)

Putting up the posters, the Guerilla Girls said later, "We felt like Robin Hood. Or Wonder Woman."

Guerrilla Girls on the prowl....

In a nearby café they put up another poster, listing the names of art galleries in the city where they and other women artists like them hoped to show their work: "These galleries show no more than 10% women or none at all."

Among many other things, New York City is a center for the arts, with numerous important art museums: the Metropolitan Museum of Art, the Museum of Modern Art, the Whitney Museum of American Art, the Brooklyn Museum and others. Hundreds of private art galleries complement these institutions.

The Guerilla Girls. They're tons of fun. They're deadly serious.

And they're definitely out there. In fact, they travel all over the world. They do all sorts of things to get attention. That's their aim and delight. Why? To see that women in the arts and women of color get equal opportunities. Their motto: "Fighting discrimination with facts, humor, and fake fur!"

The Guerrilla Girls got their start by accident, however, in fact by failing....

The posters were Act II in their story.

Act I was a flop. The Guerrilla Girls first popped up in May, 1985 to protest an exhibition at New York City's famous Museum of Modern Art (MOMA). The museum had just reopened after an extensive renovation. To celebrate, and to show it was still hip to new art, MOMA was presenting "An International Survey of Recent Painting and Sculpture." The show featured one hundred sixty-five "important" artists. The press release crowed, "The exhibition will explore the richness and diversity of recent artistic production, revealing its high quality and extraordinary vitality." However, a group of seven women artists noticed the exhibition was not really diverse. Only thirteen artists were female, just 7.87% of the painters and sculptors represented. Even fewer were artists of color.

MOMA is located on 53rd Street between Fifth and Sixth Avenues, near Rock- efeller Center and St. Patrick's Cathedral. A stone's throw from Tiffany's. In short, a prime, central location in New York City. Accordingly the seven women made protest signs. They walked up and down the sidewalk on the day the show opened, right in front of the museum's entrance, a bank of glass doors. They chanted slogans. Visitors couldn't miss them. But few people stopped to speak to them. No one refused to go in. The museum didn't add women to the show. It didn't address the issue in a public statement or press release. After a few hours, the disappointed women took their signs home.

Their effort had little effect. What to do next?

They gathered in the basement studio they shared and talked and consid- ered... and organized formally, inviting other women in the arts to join them. They saw themselves as an underground army in a war to make the arts inclu- sive.

And they got masks: "We were Guerrillas before we were Gorillas.... No one remembers, for sure, how we got our fur, but one story is that at an early meeting, an original girl, a bad speller, wrote 'Gorilla' instead of 'Guerrilla.' It was an enlightened mistake."

Then out they went, on their first night poster raid.

As one Guerrilla Girl later explained, "I completely recommend it. If you're in a situation where you're a little afraid to speak up, put a mask on. You won't believe what comes out of your mouth."

The Guerrilla Girls use a lot of humor. One poster proclaims, tongue in cheek, the "advantages" of being a woman artist, including "working without the pressure of success; knowing your career might pick up after you're 80; getting your picture in the art magazines wearing a gorilla suit."

The Guerrilla Girls' first color poster, bright yellow, remains their most iconic. It appeared in their 1989 protest against the Metropolitan Museum, using data from a self-described "weenie count" at the institution. In response to the overwhelming number of female nudes (but not female artists) the Guerrilla Girls found at the museum, the poster asked the intentionally provocative question, *"Do women have to be naked to get into the Met. Museum?"* Accompanying the words was a reproduction of French artist Jean Auguste Ingres' painting *La Grande Odalisque*, showing a reclining nude woman from behind.

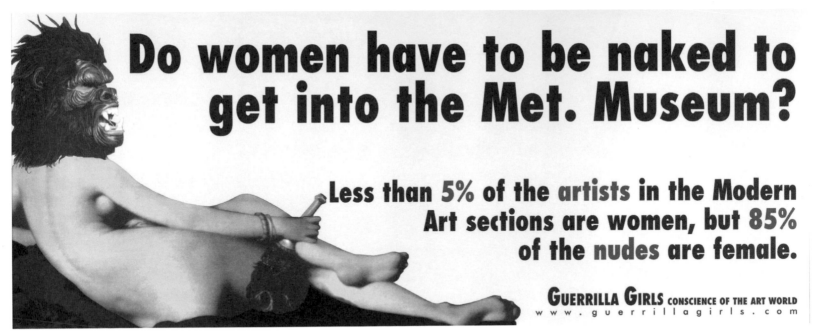

Bus poster, *Do women have to be naked to get into the Metropolitan Museum?*

Of course, on the poster the Guerrilla Girls gave her a gorilla mask. Below her a comment noted, "Less than 5% of the artists in the Modern Art sections are women, but 85% of the nudes are female."

The Guerrilla Girls created the poster as a billboard for New York's Public Art Fund, but the Fund found it offensive and rejected it. So, the Guerrilla Girls recall, "We then rented advertising space on NYC buses and ran it ourselves, until the bus company cancelled our lease, saying that the image... was too suggestive." People called to complain about the nudity. The bus company didn't want to antagonize the museum, which advertised its exhibitions on their buses. But of course the sudden cancellation made news. So more people paid attention. Success!

On their website the Guerrilla Girls describe themselves as "feminist masked avengers in the tradition of anonymous do-gooders like Robin Hood, Wonder Woman and Batman. Over 55 [actually closer to 100] women have been members over the years, some for months, some for decades." Traveling all over the U. S. and the world, they have appeared at colleges and museums in thirty-eight states and the UK, France, Australia, Brazil, Spain, Sweden, Finland, Switzerland, Poland, Ireland, Canada, and Argentina.

A 1993 travel story the Guerrilla Girls tell: "We were flown to Berlin by the cultural advisor on women's affairs to organize a protest against the exclusion of women and artists of color in the exhibition 'American Art in the 20th Century.' We snuck into the reception in full gorilla regalia, accompanied by a bunch of supporters wearing paper gorilla masks that we had supplied. We headed straight for the mayor of Berlin, who was making a speech. Security guards drew their guns. We presented the mayor with a bunch of bananas and a few choice words about sexism and racism. He smiled. The guards looked relieved."

In 1998 the group published their best-selling book, *The Guerrilla Girls' Bedside Companion to the History of Western Art*, to give neglected women artists of the past the attention they deserve. The book was lighthearted as well as informative. "We use humor to prove that feminists can be funny," the authors unapologetically explained.

In 2001 the group split into three independent entities: Guerrilla Girls on Tour, a traveling theater collective; Guerrilla Girls BroadBand, handling digital media; and Guerrilla Girls, Inc., a continuation of the original art group.

In 2006 Guerrilla Girls, Inc. joined with a Hollywood organization called Movies by Women to fund a billboard on Sunset Boulevard, just before the Academy Awards. Featuring an image of King Kong in chains, it demanded, in huge block letters: "Unchain the Women Directors!" The billboard noted that "women directed only 7% of the top 200 films of 2005, no woman director has ever won the Oscar, and only 3 have been nominated." (Lina Wertmuller, in 1976, for *Seven Beauties*; Jane Campion, in 1993, for *The Piano*; and Sofia Coppola, in 2003, for *Lost in Translation*.)

A Guerrilla Girls' press release also noted that "Only 3% of the Oscars for acting have been won by people of color. In the 21st century, low, low, low numbers like this HAVE to be the result of discrimination, unconscious, conscious or both." The Guerrilla Girls paid for another billboard showing a "replacement" Academy Award statue, The Anatomically Correct Oscar: "He's white and male, just like the guys who win."

In 2009 Kathryn Bigelow became the first woman director to win an Oscar with *The Hurt Locker*.

In addition to posters, publications, billboards, and appearances, the Guerrilla Girls participate in Amnesty International's "Stop Violence Against Women" campaign. They joined the Women's March in Washington, D.C. on January 21, 2017. In May of that year they unveiled a new poster in Bologna, Italy. "FREE THE WOMEN ARTISTS OF EUROPE!" it shouted in large pink letters. "Museums keep them locked in the basement, in storage, out of sight. Make museums show more art by women now!"

The Guerrilla Girls call themselves the "conscience of the art world." Indeed, they are. Their influence has expanded mightily since the day when the original seven women picketed MOMA. As one Guerrilla Girl said recently in a talk at that very museum, "Take a look at the woman next to you. She just might be a Guerrilla Girl. We are everywhere."

ACKNOWLEDGMENTS

Thanks to the many people who encouraged the idea of this book and reviewed drafts, *Heroic Women of the Art World* does much better justice to its subjects than it would have in my hands alone.

I thank especially early readers and immensely helpful critics Channing Frick, Peter Graham, Edwin Hagenstein, Lili Wright, and the astute and important members of Walden Writers (Pendred Noyce, Melissa Roberts, Karen Roehr, and Linda Booth Sweeney). Sarah Davies of Greenhouse Literary Agency was a key advocate.

For inspiration and support, Joseph Dobson, Ellen Feld, Beverly Freeman, Davye Gould, Trisha Leaver, Shifra Levine, Sara Macaulay, Linda Mulley, Bici Pettit-Baron, Alice F. Stern, Lydia Vagts (crucial technical advice), and Susan B. Whitlock were important. My own writing family members, Daniel Pool and Felicity Pool, were essential allies. I cannot forget past literary guides Molly Flender, Peyton Houston, Sonia Landes, Fifi Oscard, Angeline Pool, and J. Lawrence Pool.

Important material was kindly supplied by the Département des Études chinoises - Université Jean Moulin Lyon 3, établissement propriétaire du fonds de l'Institut franco-chinois de Lyon and the Bibliothèque municipale de Lyon, Fonds chinois, dépositaire du fonds de l'Institut franco-chinois de Lyon.

The many illustrations would not have been possible without the generous support of Holly Ambler, Vince Canzoneri, Jody Dobson, Parrish Dobson, Nancy Driggs, Ellen Feld, Brian Ford, Anne Garvey, Peggy Gilbert, Michael Gould, Thom Haia, Robert Harding, Victor Henningsen, Eileen Hershenov, Sonia James, Wyn Kelley, Holly Knauert, Deborah Lee, Nan Lee, Leo Liu, Lenore and Elliot Lobel, Susan Marsh, Ashley Mason, Susan McCaslin, Gabriel Mulley, Linda Mulley, David O'Neill, Lucius Palmer, Daniel Pool, Bici Pettit-Baron, Barbara Plimpton, Giridhar Ramakrishnan, Melissa Roberts, Vaughn Sills, Nick Smith, Alice F. Stern, Linda Booth Sweeney, Howard Ware, Irene Weigel, Susan Whitlock, and Janet Williamson. I am very grateful for their strong and early commitment to the book and the cause. Thank you!

Penny Noyce was an extraordinary editor (also my publisher), improving my efforts throughout. Yu-Yi Ling could answer absolutely any editorial question.

Finally, I owe so much to the two most important women in my life, each a fine writer and artist in her own right, my daughter Miranda Pool and my wife Parrish Dobson.

E. H. Pool

BIBLIOGRAPHY

ANGUISSOLA

Chadwick, Whitney. Women, Art and Society, 2nd Ed. Thames and Hudson, London, 1997, pp. 77-86.

"Excerpts from Vasari's Description of Sofonisba Anguissola." Taken from:Giorgio Vasari, The Lives of the Most Eminent Painters, Sculptors, and Architects, trans. Gaston du C. de Vere (London: Philip Lee Warner, 1912–4), V: 127–8, Web. 27 Mar. 2015. < http://italianrenaissanceresources.com/ >

Kleiner, Fred. Gardner's Art Through the Ages: A Concise Global History. Cengage Learning, 2008, 275. Web. 26 Mar. 2015.< http://books.google.com/ >

Perlingieri, Ilya Sandra. Sofonisba Anguissola: The First Great Woman Artist of the Renaissance. Rizzoli, New York, 1992.

"Sofonisba Anguissola and Others," This Web Site Created and Maintained by Adrienne De Angelis. Web. 27 Mar. 2015.< http://members.efn.org/ >

Weidemann, Christiane; Larass, Petra; and Klier, Melanie. 50 Women Artists You Should Know. Prestel, Munich, London, New York. 2008., pp. 14-17.

BALLESTRAZZI

Ballestrazzi, Mireille and Paul Katz. Madame la Commissaire. Presses de la Cité, Paris, 1999. Excerpted in Enquêtes et Témoinages, Selection du Reader's Digest, Zurich, 2001.

Ballestrazzi, Mireille and Paul Katz. Madame la Commissaire. Presses de la Cité, Paris, 1999.

Bordenave, Yves. "Meet Madame Super Cop: Mireille Ballestrazzi Is Interpol's First Ever Woman Chief," Le Monde, November 13, 2012. Web. November 18, 2014.< http://www.worldcrunch.com/ >

Cook, Don. "9 Masterworks, 5 by Monet, Seized in Paris," Los Angeles Times, October 28, 1985. Web. November 18, 2014. <http://articles.latimes.com/ >

"French Woman Elected Interpol's First Female Chief," France 24, November 11, 2012 Web. November 18, 2014. < http://www.france24.com/ >

Ganley, Elaine. "Gunmen Stage Spectacular Museum Holdup; Vanish with Art Worth $12.5 Million." Associated Press, October 28, 1985. Web. November 18, 2014. <http://apnewsarchive.com/>

Hayt-Atkins, Elizabeth. "The Japanese-French Connection." IFARreports, Vol. 8, No. 10, December 1987.

Riding, Alan. "1990 Impressionist Paintings Recovered in Corsica," The New York Times, December 7, 1990. Web. November 18, 2014. <http://nytimes.com/>

BARCILON

Barcilon, Pinin Brambilla and Marani, Pietro C. (Harlowe Tighe, Tr.). Leonardo, The Last Supper. University of Chicago Press, Chicago, 2001. (341--uneven surface)

Daley, Michael. "The 'World's Worst Restoration' and the Death of Authenticity." ArtWatch UK Online, 2012. http://artwatch.org.uk/tag/pinin-brambilla-barcilon/(newspaper critic and Prof. Zanardi)

King, Ross. Leonardo and the Last Supper. Walker & Co., New York, 2012.

Larson, Kay. "The Latest Supper." New York, 13 Feb. 1984. Web.10 Apr. 2015.

Masoero, Ada. "Sono Una Lombardaccia." Il Giornale dell' Arte, Number 351, March 2015. <https://www.ilgiornaledellarte.com/articoli/2015/3/123374.html>

Shulman, Ken. "Monumental Toil to Restore the Magnificent." The New York Times, 2 July 1995. Web. 10 Apr. 2015. < http:/nytimes.com/ >

BONHEUR

Ashton, Dore. Rosa Bonheur: A Life and a Legend. Viking Press, New York, 1981.

Klumpke, Anna. Rosa Bonheur: The Artist's (Auto)biography. University of Michigan Press, Ann Arbor, 2001, 204.

"Rosa Bonheur." Web. 25 Sep. 2015. <http://arthistoryarchive.com/>

Stanton, Theodore, Ed. Reminiscences of Rosa Bonheur. Andrew Melrose, London, 1910.

GENTILESCHI

Bissell, R. Ward. Artemisia Gentileschi and the Authority of Art: Critical Reading and
Catalogue Raisonné, Penn State University Press, State College, 1999.

Chadwick, Whitney. Women, Art and Society. 2nd Ed. Thames & Hudson, New York, 1997.

Cohen, Elizabeth S. "The Trials of Artemisia Gentileschi: A Rape as History." The Sixteenth Century Journal,

Vol. 31, No. 1, Special Edition: Gender in Early Modern Europe (Spring, 2000).

DiCaprio, Lisa and Wiesner, Merry E. Lives and Voices: Sources in European Women's History, Houghton Mifflin, New York, 2000,

Garrard, Mary. Artemisia Gentileschi: The Image of the Female Hero in Italian Baroque Art. Princeton University Press, Princeton, NJ, 1989.

GUERRILLA GIRLS

"Confessions of the Guerrilla Girls: Stories by Members 1985-2013." Web. 16 Mar. 2015. <http://guerrillagirls.com/>

"Guerrilla Girls vs. King Kong." Mark Vallen's Art For a Change, 5 Feb. 2006. Web. 16 Mar. 2015. <http://art-for-a-change.com/>

Melena Ryzik, "The Guerilla Girls, After Three Decades, Still Rattling Art World Cages." New York Times, 5 Aug. 2015. Web. 9 Dec. 2015.

HADID

"Architectural Spectacle Transforms Seoul." CNN, 3 Jun. 2014. Web. 30 May 2015.<http://edition.cnn.com/>

"Azerbaijan's Amazing Transformation," Discovery Channel. YouTube, 14 Jun. 2014. Web. 29 May 2015.

Brooks, Xan. Interview: "Zaha Hadid: 'I don't make nice little buildings.'" 22 Sep 2013.<https://www.theguardian.com/>

Qureshi, Huma. Interview: "Being an Arab and a woman is a double-edged sword." 14 Nov 2012. The Guardian. <https://www.theguardian.com/> (on the go)

Rowland, Paul. "Award-Winning Businesswomen Zaha Hadid Hits Out at 'Prejudice' Over Doomed Cardiff Bay Opera House Project," Wales Online, 23 Apr. 2013. Web. 7 Dec. 2017. <http://walesonline.co.uk/>

"The Story of Wangling SOHO: Exclusive Dialog with Zhang Xin and Zaha Hadid," SOHO China. YouTube, 8 Oct. 2014. Web. 31 May 2015.

"Who Dares, Wins: Zaha Hadid," BBC Scotland. YouTube, 2 Jan. 2014. Web. 31 May 2015.

"Zaha Hadid." Encyclopedia of World Biography. Web. 31 May 2015.

< http://notablebiographies.com/ >

HOLZER

"Jenny Holzer," Web. 4 Dec. 2017. <http://theartstory.org/>

"Jenny Holzer's Lightboard for Times Square," SFMOMA on the go. Dec. 2000. Web. 5 Oct. 2015. Web. <http://sfmoma.org/>

Pasternak, Anne. "For New York City," Creative Time: The Book. Princeton Architectural Press, Princeton, NJ, 2007.

Yau, Jon and Jackson, Shelley. "An Interview with Kenny Holzer," 6 Sep. 2006. Web. 6 Oct. 2015. <http://poetry-foundation.org/>

KAHLO

Ankori, Gannit. Frida Kahlo. Reaktion Books, London, 2013.

Grimberg, Salomon. Frida Kahlo: Song of Herself. Merrell, London, New York. n.d.

Herrera, Hayden. Frida:A Biography of Frida Kahlo. Harper Perennial, New York, 2002.

Kettenmann, Andrea. Kahlo. Taschen, New York, 1999.

Rogers, Lisa Waller. "Frida's First Bad Accident," Lisa's History Room, 26 May 2009. <http://lisawallerrogers.com>

LEIBOVITZ

Barnes, Brook. "A Topless Photo Threatens a Major Disney Franchise,"New York Times, 28 April 2008. Web. 18 Dec. 2014. <http://nytimes.com/>

Bresler, Edie. "Moments of Empathy," Life, Liberty, and Lottery. Web. 17 Dec. 2014. <https://ediebresler.word-press.com/>

Delano, Sharon, "Spotlight: Panoramic Parsons," Vanity Fair, February, 1993.

Delano, Sharon, Annie Leibovitz at Work. Random House, New York, 2008.

Goldberg, Vicki. "The New Season: Art: Icon-Maker for Excessive Times," The New York Times, 8 Sep. 1991. Web. 18 Dec. 2014. <http://nytimes.com/>

Guthmann, Edward. "Love, family, celebrity, grief -- Leibovitz puts her life on display in photo memoir." The

San Francisco Chronicle, 1 Nov. 2006. Web. 17 Dec. 2014.<http://sfgate.com/>

Leibovitz, Annie. A Photographer's Life, 1990-2005. Random House, New York, 2006.

Marcou, David J., "Gaga Over a Gargoyle," Smithsonian Magazine, February, 2008.

Montagne, Renee. "Annie Leibovitz: The View Behind the Lens," NPR, 18 Nov. 2008. Web. 18 Dec. 2014. <http://npr.org/>

Nudd, Tim. "Annie Leibovitz Revisits Her Famous Photo of John Lennon and Yoko Ono," AdWeek, 18 Jun. 2013. Web. 18 Dec. 2014. <http://adweek.com/>

Rolling Stone, Issue 1299, November 2, 2017. Editor and Publisher, Jan S. Wenner. 1290 Avenue of the Americas, New York, NY.

Wenn.com. "Annie Leibovitz: 'Miley Cyrus Photos Were Misinterpreted'", 28 Apr. 2008. Web. 26 Jan. 2015. <http://hollywood.com/>

LIN

Lin, Maya. Boundaries. Simon & Schuster, New York, 2000.

Lin, Maya. "Topologies--Process and Projects," President's Women of Yale Lecture Series, 7 Oct. 2016, president.yale.edu. Web. 21 Sep. 2017.

Maya Lin: A Strong Clear Vision. Dir: Freida Lee Mock. New Video, 1994. DVD.

Menand, Louis. "Maya Lin and the Vietnam Veterans Memorial," American Studies, Farrar, Straus and Giroux, New York, 2003, excerpt posted on The History Reader, 27 Mar 2012. Web. 2 Mar. 2015.

Menand, Louis. "The Reluctant Memorialist," 8 Jul. 2002. Web. 27 Nov. 2015. <http://qqq.cuny.edu/>

Moyers, Bill. "Public Affairs Television 'Becoming American' Interview with Maya Lin, 2003. Web. 27 Feb. 2015. <http://pbs.org/>

Scruggs, Jan C. and Joel L. Swerdlow. To Heal a Nation: The Vietnam Veterans Memorial. Harper & Row, New York, 1985

MORISOT

Amiot-Saulnier, Emmanuelle. "Manet et Ses Muses," Manet au Musée d'Orsay, Éditions Faton, Dijon, 2011, pp.44-55.

Higonnet, Anne. Berthe Morisot. University of California Press, Berkeley, 1995.

"Berthe Morisot," Renoir Fine Art, Inc. Web. 5 Mar. 2013. <http://renoirinc.com/>

Roberts, Rosalind de Boland and Jane. Growing Up with the Impressionists: The Diary of Julie Manet. Sotheby's Publications, London, 1987.

Rouart, Dennis, Ed. Berthe Morisot: Correspondence. Moyer Bell, Mount Kisco, NY, 1987.

Stuckey, Charles F.; Scott, William P.; Lindsay, Suzanne G. Berthe Morisot: Impressionist. Hudson Hills Press, New York, 1987.

PAN

"A Lonely Legacy of Pan Yuliang." China Daily, 5 Sep 2007. Web. 21 Jan. 2019. < http://china.org.cn/ >

Clark, John. "Pan Yuliang Chronology." The Asian Modern. 2013. Web. 23 Jan. 2019. <http://cdn.aaa.org.hk/_source/digital_collection/fedora_extracted/45815.pdf/>

Croizier, Ralph. "Pan Yuliang." Biographical Dictionary of Chinese Women: The Twentieth Century, 1912-2000, M. E. Sharpe, 2003, p. 419.

"Pan Yuliang: A Journey to Silence." Nikita Yongqian Cai, at Villa Vassilieff. 8 Mar. 2017. Web 23 Jan, 2019. <http://www.villavassilieff.net/?-Pan-Yuliang-A-Journey-to-Silence-149-/>

Teo, Phyllis. Rewriting Modernism: Three Women Artists in Twentieth-Century China. Leiden University Press, Leiden, 2016.

YouTube, "The Works: Chinese female artists Pan Yuliang and Cao Fei." Published 3 Oct. 2018. Web. 23 Jan. 2019. <https://www.youtube.com/

RINGGOLD

"Faith Ringgold's Artist Statement." Web. 19 May 2015. < http:// faithringgold.blogspot.com/ >

Farrington, Lisa E. Faith Ringgold. Pomegranate, San Francisco, 2004.

"Geary Gallery of Darien," Purchase, NY. Web. 4 May 2015. <http://artdaily.com/>

Ringgold, Faith. We Flew Over the Bridge: The Memoirs of Faith Ringgold. Little Brown & Co., Boston, 1995.

Russeth, Andrew. "The Storyteller," ArtNews, Spring, 2016. Web. 1 Mar 2016. <www.artnews.com>

"Students' and artists' protest letter to Bates Lowry, New York, N.Y., ca. 1969." Archives of American Art. Web.

20 May 2015. <http://aaa.si.edu/>

Wallace, Michele. "Soul Pictures: Black Feminist Generations." Web. 19 May 2015. <http://mjsoulpictures.blog-spot.com/>

SAVAGE

Alexander, Kaylee. "Augusta Savage, LENORE," 3 Jun. 2014. Web. 21 Mar. 2015.<http://crssculpture.org/>

Augusta Savage. Bio. A&E Television Network, 2015. Web. 19 Mar. 2015.

"Augusta Savage," Department of State Division of Cultural Affairs Programs, Florida Artists Hall of Fame. dos.myflorida.com. Web. 19 Mar. 2015.

Foster, Katherine D. "Augusta Savage." Web. 21 Mar. 2015. <http://blackpast.org/>

Gates, Henry and Higginbotham, Evelyn Brooks. "Augusta Savage." Harlem Lives for the African American National Biography. Oxford Univ. Press, New York, 2009.

Mauer, Amanda. "Augusta Savage," YouTube, 19 Nov. 2011. Web. 20 Mar. 2015.

Oral history interview with Norman Lewis, 1968 July 14, Archives of American Art, Smithsonian Institution. Web. 20 Mar. 2105. <http://aaa.si.edu/>

Oral history interview with Jacob Lawrence, 1968 Oct. 26, Archives of American Art, Smithsonian Institution. Web. 20 Mar. 2015. <http://aaa.si.edu/ >

Pedersen, Ginger L. "Hands of Creation: Augusta Christine Savage," 27 Nov. 2011. Web. 19 Mar. 2015. <http:// palmbeachpast.org/>

Perry, Regenia A. Free within Ourselves: African-American Artists in the Collection of the National Museum of American Art (Washington, D.C.: National Museum of American Art in Association with Pomegranate Art Books, 1992). Web. 19 Mar. 2015. <http://americanart.si.edu/>

Poston, T. R. "Augusta Savage," Metropolitan Magazine, Jan. 1935, n.p. Web. 20 Mar. 2105. <http://americanart.si.edu/>

Schroeder, Alan and Bereal, JaeMe. In Her Hands:The Story of Sculptor Augusta Savage. Lee & Low Books, New York, 2009.

Sherry. "Memories of Augusta Savage in Saugerties," 14 Oct. 2010. Web. 20 Mar. 2015.<http://myauctionfinds.com/>

Weiss, Glenn. "Idea: Recast Augusta Savage's 1939 World's Fair Sculpture." 10 Jan. 2015. Web. 19 Mar. 2015.

<http://ibiartwestpalm.wordpress.com/>

VALLAND

Bouchoux, Corinne and Edsel, Robert M. Rose Valland:Resistance at the Museum. Laurel Publishing, Dallas, TX, 2013.

Dörman, Knut.Elements of War Crimes under the Rome Statute of the International Criminal Court,Cambridge Univ. Press, New York, 2003.

Edsel, Robert M. with Bret Witter. The Monuments Men: Allied Heroes, Nazi Thieves, and the Greatest Treasure Hunt in History. Center Street, New York, 2009.

Nicholas, Lynn H. The Rape of Europa: The Fate of Europe's Treasures in the Third Reich and the Second World War. Alfred A. Knopf, New York, 1994, p. 125.

Office of Strategic Services Art Looting Investigation Unit APO 413, U.S. Army Consolidated Interrogation Report No. 1, 15 August 1945. Web. 9 Nov. 2014. <http://lootedart.com/>

Schwartz, Claire. "Saving a Bit of Beauty for the World: Retelling the Story of Rose Valland." Dominican University of California, 2016 Interdisciplinary Writing Award.

Valland, Rose. Le Front de L'Art: Défense des Collections Françaises, 1939-1945.

(M) Réunion des MuséesNationaux, Paris, 2016.

VIGÉE LEBRUN

Evans, Siân. The Memoirs of Elisabeth VigéeLeBrun. Camden Press, London, 1989.

May, Gita. ElisabethVigéeLeBrun: The Odyssey of an Artist in an Age of Revolution.

Yale University Press, New Haven and London, 2005.

IMAGE CREDITS

Chapter 3

Chapter 4

https://upload.wikimedia.org/wikipedia/commons/6/6c/Rosa_Bonheur_-_Indiens_%C3%A0_cheval_arm%C3%A9s_de_lances.jpg Rosa Bonheur [Public domain]

Chapter 5

https://upload.wikimedia.org/wikipedia/commons/2/2c/Edouard_Manet_-_Berthe_Morisot_With_a_Bouquet_of_Violets_-_Google_Art_Project.jpg [public domain]

https://upload.wikimedia.org/wikipedia/commons/6/67/Berthe_Morisot_-_Reading_%28La_Lecture%29.jpg Berthe Morisot [Public domain]

https://upload.wikimedia.org/wikipedia/commons/b/b7/Berthe_Morisot_-_Sommertag_-_1879.jpeg Berthe Morisot [Public domain]

https://upload.wikimedia.org/wikipedia/commons/0/02/%C3%89douard_Manet_-_Le_repos.jpg Édouard Manet [Public domain]

https://upload.wikimedia.org/wikipedia/commons/c/ca/Berthe_Morisot_-_The_Cradle_-_Google_Art_Project.jpg Berthe Morisot [Public domain]

https://upload.wikimedia.org/wikipedia/commons/3/33/Eugene_Manet_and_His_Daughter_at_Bougival_1881_Berthe_Morisot.jpg Berthe Morisot [Public domain]

Chapter 6

'Lift Ev'ry Voice and Sing,' New York World's Fair, Manuscripts and Archives Division, The New York Public Library

1939 New York World's Fair by Sherman Oaks Antique Mall/ GettyImage

Augusta Savage with her sculpture Realization, circa 1938 / Andrew Herman, photographer. Federal Art Project, Photographic Division collection, circa 1920-1965, bulk 1935-1942. Archives of American Art, Smithsonian Institution.

AUGUSTA SAVAGE (1892-1962). Courtesy: CSU Archives / Everett Collection Historical / Alamy Stock Photo

https://commons.wikimedia.org/wiki/File:Archives_of_American_Art_-_Augusta_Savage_-_2371.jpg Archives of American Art [Public domain]

Gamin https://americanart.si.edu/artwork/gamin-21658

https://upload.wikimedia.org/wikipedia/commons/8/8e/1august_fells.jpg «Marylandstater» «reply» at English Wikipedia. [Public domain]

Chapter 7

Pan yuliang self portrait 1924, Historic Collection / Alamy Stock Photo

https://www.bm-lyon.fr/IMG/jpg/825-01.jpg, Didier Nicole, BML, with permission of Bibliotheque municipal de Lyon

Woman looking backwards, collection of Anhui Museum, with permission of Anhui Museum

Self portrait with flowers, collection of Anhui Museum, with permission of Anhui Museum

https://upload.wikimedia.org/wikipedia/commons/1/13/Mao_Tse-Tung%2C_leader_of_China%27s_Communists%2C_addresses_some_of_his_followers._-_NARA_-_196235.jpg National Archives and Records Administration [Public domain]

https://upload.wikimedia.org/wikipedia/commons/7/73/Frederick_Carl_Frieseke%2C_1900c_-_Montparnasse_Landscape.jpg Frederick Carl Frieseke [Public domain]

Chapter 8

https://commons.wikimedia.org/wiki/File:Statue_Rose_Valland.jpg, Projectim [CC BY-SA 4.0 (https://creativecommons.org/licenses/by-sa/4.0)]

https://upload.wikimedia.org/wikipedia/commons/a/a9/Front_of_the_Galerie_nationale_du_Jeu_de_Paume_in_Tuileries_Gardens_in_Paris.jpg TCY [CC BY-SA 3.0 (http://creativecommons.org/licenses/by-sa/3.0/)]

https://www.artrecovery.com/gurlitt-hoard

http://www.a-fresco.com/fresque/rose-valland/ Rose Valland, fresque réalisée à Saint-Etienne de Saint Geoirs, France par A-FRESCO.com

Movie poster The Train (1964) AF archive / Alamy Stock Photo

https://upload.wikimedia.org/wikipedia/commons/7/78/Crowds_of_French_patriots_line_the_Champs_Elysees-edit2.jpg [public domain]

Rose Valland, a French Art Historian, secretly recorded details of the Nazi art plundering. Everett Collection Historical / Alamy Stock Photo

https://www.si.edu/object/AAADCD_item_15137

https://upload.wikimedia.org/wikipedia/commons/5/53/Plaque_Rose_Valland_-_Cropped.jpg User:TCY, Attribution-ShareAlike 3.0 Unported (CC BY-SA 3.0)

Chapter 9

Self-Portrait, Thorn Necklace, Harry Ransom Center, The University of Texas at Austin

https://upload.wikimedia.org/wikipedia/commons/a/a4/A_thangka_%28religious_painting%29%2C_School_of_Traditional_Arts%2C_Thimphu.jpg Stephen Shephard [CC BY-SA 3.0 (http://creativecommons.org/licenses/by-sa/3.0/)]

"'Tar Beach' quilt, showing Cassie soaring over the George Washington Bridge." © 2019 Faith Ringgold/Artists Rights Society (ARS), New York, Courtesy ACA

https://commons.wikimedia.org/wiki/File:Tar_Beach_(2)_PMA_(10)_(25144975369).jpg, Regan Vercruysse from Stewartsville, New Jersey, USA [CC BY 2.0 (https://creativecommons.org/licenses/by/2.0)]

Chapter 12

https://upload.wikimedia.org/wikipedia/commons/7/71/Annie_Leibovitz-SF-1-Crop.jpg Robert Scoble from Half Moon Bay, USA [CC BY 2.0 (https://creativecommons.org/licenses/by/2.0)]

https://upload.wikimedia.org/wikipedia/commons/0/05/Chrysler_Building_Eagles_left.jpg twitter.com/mat-twi1son from England [CC BY 2.0 (https://creativecommons.org/licenses/by/2.0)]

US photographer, Annie Leibovitz unveils her new exhibition 'Women: New Portraits', at the Wapping Hydraulic Power Station. EL pics / Alamy Stock Photo

Photographer Annie Leibovitz talks about her work, Annie. ZUMA Press, Inc. / Alamy Stock Photo

Sontag, Susan, 16.1.1933 - 28.12.2004, American author / writer, half length, May 1993, INTERFOTO / Alamy Stock Photo

https://commons.wikimedia.org/wiki/File:Obama_family_portrait_in_the_Green_Room.jpg Annie Leibovitz / Released by White House Photo Office [Public domain]

Chapter 13

"Holzer's message on abuse of power in Times Square." Photo credit: courtesy: Jenny Holzer, Art Resource, NY

Miami Florida Perez Art Museum Miami PAMM gallery contemporary inside artist, Jenny Holzer Inflammatory Essays. Photo credit: Jeff Greenberg / Alamy Stock Photo

Bilbao Museo Guggenheim Installation for Bilbao (Jenny Holzer) 5, Archive PL / Alamy Stock Photo

I breathe, photo by Phillipp Scholz Rittermann

US artist Jenny Holzer smiles in front of her installation 'Red Tilt' in the museum in Goslar, Germany, dpa picture alliance / Alamy Stock Photo

Chapter 14

https://www.flickr.com/photos/eager/16987626272 Zaha Hadid Portrait by Steve Double 01, Attribution 2.0 Generic (CC BY 2.0)

https://upload.wikimedia.org/wikipedia/commons/e/e4/Heydar_Aliyev_Center.jpg Asif Masimov [CC BY-SA 4.0 (https://creativecommons.org/licenses/by-sa/4.0)]

thttps://zh.wikipedia.org/wiki/%E5%B9%BF%E5%B7%9E%E5%A4%A7%E5%89%A7%E9%99%A2#/media/File:Guangzhou_Opera_House(Near).JPG Mr a [CC BY 3.0 (https://creativecommons.org/licenses/by/3.0)]

https://upload.wikimedia.org/wikipedia/commons/e/e4/MSU_Broad_Art_Museum_exterior_1.jpg Dj1997 [CC BY-SA 3.0 (https://creativecommons.org/licenses/by-sa/3.0)]

https://commons.wikimedia.org/wiki/File:Dongdaemun_Design_Plaza.jpg Warren Whyte [CC BY-SA 4.0 (https://creativecommons.org/licenses/by-sa/4.0)]

Chapter 15

https://upload.wikimedia.org/wikipedia/commons/thumb/5/59/Monet_-_Impression%2C_Sunrise.jpg/2048px-Monet_-_Impression%2C_Sunrise.jpg Claude Monet [Public domain]

https://upload.wikimedia.org/wikipedia/commons/4/49/Mireille_Ballestrazzi_Interpol%2C_Colombia_%2810410710804%29_%28cropped%29.jpg National Police of Colombia [CC BY-SA 2.0 (https://creativecommons.org/licenses/by-sa/2.0)]

https://upload.wikimedia.org/wikipedia/commons/6/69/Pont_Pinard_%28Semur-en-Auxois%29_15-08-2006.JPG, Renaud MAVRÉ, public domain

https://commons.wikimedia.org/wiki/File:Jean-Baptiste_C._Corot_-_The_fisherman-_evening_effect_-_Google_Art_Project.jpg Art Gallery of South Australia [Public domain]

https://upload.wikimedia.org/wikipedia/commons/6/63/Genoise_tower_in_corsica.jpg Tanos [CC BY-SA 2.0 fr (https://creativecommons.org/licenses/by-sa/2.0/fr/deed.en)]

https://upload.wikimedia.org/wikipedia/commons/5/53/Berthe_Morisot_Jeune_fille_au_bal.jpg Berthe Morisot [Public domain]

https://www.gettyimages.com/detail/news-photo/commissary-mireille-ballestrazzi-and-her-team-with-news-photo/543894164, Police Team with Stolen Artworks by Antoine Gyori – Corbis/GettyImage

Chapter 16

https://upload.wikimedia.org/wikipedia/commons/1/17/Maya_Lin_1.JPG Sharon Styer [CC BY-SA 3.0 (http://creativecommons.org/licenses/by-sa/3.0/)]

Chapter 17

ABOUT THE AUTHOR

EUGENE POOL is a teacher and writer who grew up among beautiful paintings by Mary Cassatt, Vieira da Silva, Lee Krasner, Picasso, Modigliani, and others. He studied art history at Harvard and later studied both architectural design and painting. He has taught both English and Art History at Buckingham Browne & Nichols and the Winsor School, two of the nation's top independent schools. At the Winsor School, which is all girls, he won the school's top teaching award.